The Connection Machine

ACM Distinguished Dissertations

The Connection Machine
W. Daniel Hillis

The MIT Press
Cambridge, Massachusetts
London, England

Sixth printing, 1992

First MIT Press paperback edition, 1989

This book was set using LaTEX by Thinking Machines Corporation and printed and bound by Halliday Lithograph in the United States of America. The terms in the index were selected automatically using The TMC Indexer.

VAX is a trademark of Digital Equipment Corporation. Connection Machine, CmLisp, and The TMC Indexer are trademarks of Thinking Machines Corporation. Disney World is a trademark of Walt Disney Enterprises.

Library of Congress Cataloging-in-Publication Data

Hillis, W. Daniel.
  The connection machine.

(The MIT Press series in artifical intelligence)
Thesis (Ph.D.)—MIT, 1985.
Bibliography: p.
Includes index.
1. Machine theory. 2. Artificial intelligence.
I. Title. II. Series.
QA267.H487 1985   004   85–15318
ISBN 0-262-08157-1 (hardcover)
        0-262-58097-7 (paperback)

Contents

Series Foreword

This book is being published by The MIT Press as an outgrowth of the annual contest for the best doctoral dissertation in computer-related science and engineering. The contest was initiated in 1982 by the ACM in cooperation with MIT Press.

The Distinguished Doctoral Dissertation Series has been created to recognize that some of the theses considered in the final round of selecting a contest winner also deserve publication. In the judgment of the ACM selection committee, this thesis is of such high quality that it deserves special recognition in this series.

Dr. W. Daniel Hillis wrote his thesis on "The Connection Machine" at the Massachusetts Institute of Technology. The thesis was supervised by Gerald Sussman, Professor of Electrical Engineering and Computer Science. The thesis was submitted to the 1985 competition. The ACM Doctoral Dissertation Award Subcommittee recommended publication of this thesis because the Connection Machine represents a realistic alternative to classic von Neumann architecture that should make ambitious theories in artificial intelligence accessible to experimental analysis and testing. The Connection Machine is a general-purpose, massively parallel processor in which processing is integrated into and distributed through the memory so that allocation of memory to represent data automatically allocates processing for manipulation of that data. Communication among processing element is abstracted away from the programmer in a packet-switched communication. This allows Dr. Hillis to develop a low-level extension to Lisp that enables one to abstractly program a connection machine for a variety of difficult problems.

John R. White, Chairman
ACM Doctoral Dissertation Award Subcommittee

Acknowledgments

In alphabetical order:

Hal Abelson, who encouraged me to work on this in the early stages. Phil Agre, who did some of the first programming on the machine. Jim Bailey, who appreciated the elegance from the first time he heard about it and explained it to everyone else. Alan Bawden, who invented the first programming languages for the machine. Gordon Bell, who gave lots of advice that I listened to and some that I wish I had. Danny Bobrow, who took me seriously. Michael Brady, for encouragement. Keira Bromberg, who was relentless. Tom Callahan, who built it; nothing is impossible for him. David Chapman, who had the first ideas about how to make conventional programs run on the machine. Dave Christman, who invented many of the basic algorithms. Arlene Chung, for making the pictures prettier. Dick Clayton, who made it real. It never would have happened without him, really. John Cocke, for discussions on architecture. Jim Cohen, for constant support. Glen Kramer, who figured out how to use the machine for test vector generation. Marvin Denicoff, for understanding. Michael Dertouzos, who gave me the support to build my first parallel processor. Chris Drake, for good humor. Gary Drescher, for teaching me to think better. Mike Drumheller, who wrote the first vision program. Scott Fahlman, whose thesis inspired the machine. Carl Feynman, for energy, joy, and enthusiasm from the beginning. Richard Feynman, for teaching me something about what is important and what is not. Rolf-Dieter Fiebrich, who led the group that wrote the first useful programs for the machine, with a sense of wonder and excitement. Craig Fields, who knew it was the right thing. Richard Greenblatt, for advice and encouragement. Sheryl Handler, for unending confidence in me and for showing me the power and perils of positive thought. Robert Heinlein, for making me want to go to MIT. Carl Hewitt, for good discussions. John Huffman, who designed the chip. Lyman Hurd, who analyzed the router. Brewster Kahle, one of the machine's primary designers, for boundless effort, friendship and excitement, which makes it all worthwhile. Bob Kahn, who supported the machine throughout its development. John Kimberly, who designed the I/O for the prototype. Tom Knight, who was one of the principal designers of the first prototype. Bradley Kuszmaul, who figured out how to compile functional programs for the machine. Cliff Lasser, who wrote the first language that worked on the machine. Jerry Letvin, for talking me out of being a neurophysiologist. Clem Liu, who was one of the principal designers of the prototype. Pati Marx, for love and support. Antonio Marzullo, for being there when I needed him. Boris Mashalov, for keeping things apart. Neil Mayle, who wrote the initial simulations. Mirza Mehdi, for making the deals. Margaret Minsky, who helped and encouraged me, for good criticism, ideas and companionship. Marvin Minsky, my mentor, who taught me to think. Most of the ideas in the book have their root, directly or indirectly, in discussions with Marvin. (See also Thesis Committee.) The Minsky family, Julie, Henry, Margaret, Gloria and Marvin, who adopted me when I moved to Boston. Guy Montpetit for joy and his sense of the adventure. Paul Mott, for indexing on the Fourth of July. Bruce Nemnich, who made things work. William Paley, for believing in the dream. Seymour Papert, for supervising my first projects at MIT. Tom Poggio, who is my model of a true scientist. Michael Rabin, for discussions on algorithms. Howard Resnikoff, for finding order in chaos (and Sheryl Handler for the reverse). George Robertson, who wrote the first code to run on the hardware. Paul Rosenblum, who kept up the dress code. Jim Salem, who accidently wrote the router diagnostic. Jack Schwartz, who took the trouble to understand the details. Claude Shannon, whose playful spirit got the field off to a good start. (See also Thesis Committee.) Brian Silverman, for early discussions on the router. Karl Sims, who is the first person to apply the machine to graphics. Mark Stefik, for early encouragement. Steve Squires, for support, ideas, and enthusiasm. Frank Stanton, for advice and support. Guy Steele, who headed the software team for the prototype. Dave Stefanovic, who made things work. Gerald Sussman, who gave me good advice and encouragement. Many of the key early ideas came out of discussions with Gerry. (See also Thesis Committee.) Ivan Sutherland, who said to think about wires instead of switches. John Taft, who was one of the designers of the first prototype. Wati Taylor, who figured out how to do sorting. Tamiko Thiel, who made it beautiful. Umesh Vasirani, who wrote one of the initial simulations. Dave Waltz, who is applying the machine to natural language understanding. Dan Weinreb, who wrote one of the initial simulations. Debbie Widener, for writing the book. Jerry Wiesner, for encouragement and advice. Patrick Winston, who supported the work from the beginning. (See also Thesis Committee.) Steve Wolfram, for friendship, ideas, and encourgement. The people and creatures of Disney World, who guarded me while I wrote the first draft. Lowell Wood, who recognized my potential before I did but fortunately was unable to exploit it, for encouragement, humor and advice. I would also like to thank my Thesis Committee, Marvin Minsky (thesis advisor), Claude Shannon (advisor), Gerald Sussman (thesis advisor), Patrick Winston; the Defense Advanced Research Projects Agency and the Naval Electronic Systems Command for support of the construction of the prototype under contract #N00039-84-C-0638; the Fannie and John Hertz Foundation, which supported me for six long years without complaint; and the editorial staff of The MIT Press.

The book is dedicated to my family, Beth, David, Argye and Bill, for years of love and support.

The Connection Machine

Chapter 1

Introduction

1.1 We Would Like to Make a Thinking Machine

Someday, perhaps soon, we will build a machine that will be able to perform the functions of a human mind, a thinking machine. One of the many problems that must be faced in designing such a machine is the need to process large amounts of information rapidly, more rapidly than is ever likely to be possible with a conventional computer. In this book I describe a new type of computing engine called a *Connection Machine*; it computes through the interaction of many, say a million, simple identical processing/memory cells. Because the processing takes place concurrently, the Connection Machine Computer can be much faster than a traditional computer.

Our Current Machines Are Too Slow

Although the construction of an artificial intelligence is not yet within our reach, the ways in which current computer architectures fall short of the task are already evident. Consider a specific problem. Let us say that we are asked to describe, in a single sentence, the picture shown in figure 1.1. With almost no apparent difficulty a person is able to say something like "It is a group of people and horses." This is easy for us. We do it almost effortlessly. Yet for a modern digital computer it is an almost impossible task. Given such an image, the computer first has to process the hundreds of thousands of points of visual information in the picture to find the lines, the connected regions, and the textures of the shadows. From these lines and regions it then constructs some sort of three-dimensional model of the shapes of the objects and their locations in space. Then it has to match these objects against a library of known forms to recognize the faces, the hands, the folds of the hills, etc. Even this is not sufficient to make sense of the picture. Understanding the image requires a great deal of commonsense knowledge about the world. For example, to recognize the simple waving

Figure 1.1 *The Watering Place*, Pablo Picasso, 1905.

lines as hills, one needs to expect hills; to recognize horses' tails, one needs
to expect a tail at the end of a horse.

Even if the machine had this information stored in its memory, it would
probably not find it without first considering and rejecting many other pos-
sibly relevant pieces of information, such as that people often sit on chairs,
that horses can wear saddles, and that Picasso sometimes shows scenes from
multiple perspectives. As it turns out, these facts are all irrelevant for the
interpretation of this particular image, but the computer would have no a
priori method of rejecting their relevance without considering them. Once
the objects of the picture are recognized, the computer then has to formulate
a sentence which offers a concise description. This involves understanding
which details are interesting and relevant and choosing a relevant point of
view. For example, it probably would not be satisfactory to describe the

picture as "Two hills, partially obscured by lifeforms," even though this may be accurate.

We know just enough about each of these tasks so that we might plausibly undertake to program a computer to generate one-sentence descriptions of simple pictures, but the process would be tedious, and the resulting program would be extremely slow. What the human mind does almost effortlessly would take the fastest existing computers many days. These electronic giants that so outmatch us in adding columns of numbers are equally outmatched by us in the processes of symbolic thought.

The Computer versus the Brain

So what's wrong with the computer? Part of the problem is that we do not yet fully understand the algorithms of thinking. But part of the problem is speed. One might suspect that the reason the computer is slow is that its electronic components are much slower than the biological components of the brain, but this is not the case. A transistor can switch in a few nanoseconds, about a million times faster than the millisecond switching time of a neuron. A more plausible argument is that the brain has more neurons than the computer has transistors, but even this fails to explain the disparity in speed. As near as we can tell, the human brain has about 10^{10} neurons, each capable of switching no more than a thousand times a second. So the brain should be capable of about 10^{13} switching events per second. A modern digital computer, by contrast, may have as many as 10^9 transistors, each capable of switching as often as 10^9 times per second. So the total switching speed should be as high as 10^{18} events per seconds, or 10,000 times greater than the brain. Thus the sheer computational power of the computer should be much greater than that of the human. Yet we know the reality to be just the reverse. Where did the calculation go wrong?

1.2   Classical Computer Architecture Reflects Obsolete Assumptions

One reason that computers are slow is that their hardware is used extremely inefficiently. The actual number of events per second in a large computer today is less than one-tenth of one percent of the number calculated in section

1.1. The reasons for the inefficiency are partly technical but mostly historical. The basic forms of today's architectures were developed under a different set of technologies, when different assumptions from those that are appropriate today were applied. The machine described here, the Connection Machine, is an architecture that better fits today's technology and, I hope, better fits the requirements of a thinking machine.

A modern large computer contains about 1 m^2 of silicon. This square meter contains approximately one billion transistors which make up the processor and memory of the computer. The interesting point here is that both the processor and memory are made of the same stuff. This was not always the case. When von Neumann and his colleagues were designing the first computers, their processors were made of relatively fast and expensive switching components, such as vacuum tubes, whereas the memories were made of relatively slow and inexpensive components, such as delay lines or storage tubes. The result was a two-part design that kept the expensive vacuum tubes as busy as possible. We call this two-part design, with memory on one side and processing on the other, the von Neumann architecture, and it is the way that almost all computers are built today. This basic design has been so successful that most computer designers have kept it even though the technological reason for the memory/processor split no longer is justified.

The Memory/Processor Split Leads to Inefficiency

In a large von Neumann computer almost none of its billion or so transistors do any useful processing at any given instant. Almost all the transistors are in the memory section of the machine, and only a few of those memory locations are accessed at any given time. The two-part architecture keeps the silicon devoted to processing wonderfully busy, but this is only 2 or 3 percent of the silicon area. The other 97 percent sits idle. At a million dollars per square meter for processed, packaged silicon, this is an expensive resource to waste. If we were to take another measure of cost in the computer, kilometers of wire, the results would be much the same: Most of the hardware is in memory, so most of the hardware is doing nothing most of the time.

As we build larger computers, the problem becomes even worse. It is relatively straightforward to increase the size of memory in a machine, but it is far from obvious how to increase the size of the processor. The result is that as we build bigger machines with more silicon, or, equivalently, as we squeeze more transistors into each unit of area, the machines have a larger ratio of memory to processing power and are consequently even less efficient. This inefficiency remains no matter how fast we make the processor because the length of the computation becomes dominated by the time required to move data between processor and memory. This is called the von Neumann bottleneck. The bigger we build machines, the worse it gets.

1.3 Concurrency Offers a Solution

The obvious answer is to get rid of the von Neumann architecture and build a more homogeneous computing machine in which memory and processing are combined. It is not difficult today to build a machine with hundreds of thousands or even millions of tiny processing cells which has a raw computational power that is many orders of magnitude greater than the fastest conventional machines. The problem lies in how to couple the raw power with the applications of interest, how to program the hardware to the job. How do we decompose our application into hundreds of thousands of parts that can be executed concurrently? How do we coordinate the activities of a million processing elements to accomplish a single task? The Connection Machine architecture was designed as an answer to these questions.

Why do we even believe that it is possible to perform these calculations with such a high degree of concurrency? There are two reasons. First, we have the existence proof of the human brain, which manages to achieve the performance we are after with a large number of apparently slow switching components. Second, we have many specific examples in which particular computations can be achieved with high degrees of concurrency by arranging the processing elements to match the natural structure of the data.

Image Processing: One Processor per Pixel

In image processing, for example, we know that it is possible to perform two-dimensional filtering operations efficiently using a two-dimensionally connected grid of processing elements. In this application it is most natural to store each point of the image in its own processing cell. A 1000×1000 point image would use a million processors. In this case, each step of the calcu-

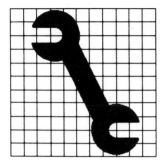 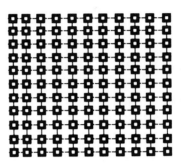

Figure 1.2 In a machine vision application, a separate processor/memory cell processes each point in the image. Because the computation is two-dimensional the processors are connected into a two-dimensional grid.

lation can be performed locally within a pixel's processor or through direct communication with the processors' two-dimensionally connected neighbors. (See figure 1.2.) A typical step of such a computation involves calculating for each point the average value of the points in the immediate neighborhood. Such averages can be computed simultaneously for all points in the image. For instance, to compute the average of each point's four immediate neighbors requires four concurrent processing steps during which each cell passes a value to the right, left, below, and above. On each of these steps the cell also receives a value from the opposite direction and adds it to its accumulated average. Four million arithmetic operations are computed in the time normally required for four.

VLSI Simulation: One Processor per Transistor

The image processing example works because the structure of the problem matches the communication structure of the cells. The application is two dimensional, the hardware is two dimensional. In other applications the natural structure of the problem is not nearly so regular and depends in detail on the data being operated on. An example of such an application outside the field of artificial intelligence is the simulation of an integrated circuit with hundreds of thousands of transistors. Such problems occur regularly in verifying the design of a very large scale integrated (VLSI) circuit. Obviously, the calculation can be done concurrently because the transistors do it concurrently. A hundred thousand transistors can be simulated by a hundred thousand processors. To do this efficiently, the processors have to be wired into the same pattern as the transistors. (See figure 1.3.) Each processor simulates a single transistor by communicating directly with processors simulating connected transistors. When a voltage changes on the gate of a transistor, the processor simulating the transistor calculates the transistor's response and communicates the change to processors simulating connected transistors. If many transistors are changing at once, then many responses are calculated concurrently, just as in the actual circuit. The natural connection pattern of the processors depends on the exact connection pattern of the circuit being simulated.

Semantic Networks: One Processor per Concept

The human brain, so far as we know, is not particularly good at simulating transistors, but it does seem to be good at solving problems that require manipulating poorly structured data. These manipulations can be performed by processors that are connected into patterns that mimic patterns of the data. For example, many artificial intelligence programs represent data in the form of *semantic networks*. A semantic network is a labeled graph in which each vertex represents a concept and each edge represents a relationship between concepts. For example, `Apple` and `Red` are represented by nodes with a `Color-of` link connecting them. (See figure 1.4.) Much of the knowledge that one might wish to extract from such a network is not represented explicitly by the links but instead must be inferred by searching for patterns that involve multiple links. For example, if we know that `My-Apple` is an `Apple`, we can infer that `My-Apple` is `Red` from the combination of the `Is-a` link between `My-Apple` and `Apple` and the `Color-of` link between `Apple` and `Red`.

In a real-world database there are hundreds of thousands of concepts

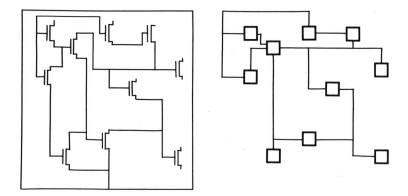

Figure 1.3 In the VLSI simulation application, a separate processor/memory cell is used to simulate each transistor. The processors are connected in the pattern of the circuit.

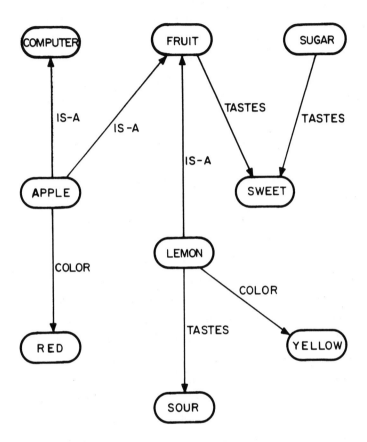

Figure 1.4 In a semantic network one processor/memory cell is used to represent each concept, and the connections between the cells represent the relationships between the concepts.

and millions of links. The inference rules are far more complex than simple `Is-a` deductions. For example, there are rules to handle exceptions, contradictions, and uncertainty. The system needs to represent and manipulate information about parts and wholes, spatial and temporal relationships, and causality. Such computations can become extremely complicated. Answering a simple commonsense question from such a database, such as "Will my apple fall if I drop it?" can take a serial computer many hours. Yet a human answers questions such as this almost instantly, so we have good reason to believe that it can be done concurrently.

This particular application, retrieving commonsense knowledge from a semantic network, was one of the primary motivations for the design of the Connection Machine. There are semantic network-based knowledge representation languages, such as NETL (Fahlman 1979), which were specifically designed to allow the deductions necessary for retrieval to be computed in parallel. In such a system each concept or assertion can be represented by its own independent processing element. Because related concepts must communicate in order to perform deductions, the corresponding processors must be connected. In this case, the topology of the hardware depends on the information stored in the network. So, for example, if `Apple` and `Red` are related, then there must be a connection between the processor representing `Apple` and the processor representing `Red` so that deductions about `Apples` can be related to deductions about `Red`. Given a collection of processors whose connection pattern matches the data stored in the network, the retrieval operations can be performed quickly and in parallel.

There are many more examples of this sort. For each, extreme concurrency can be achieved in the computation so long as the hardware is connected in such a way as to match the particular structure of the application. They could each be solved quickly on a machine that provides a large number of processing memory elements whose connection pattern can be reconfigured to match the natural structure of the application.

1.4   Deducing the Requirements from an Algorithm

I will consider a specific concurrent algorithm in detail and use it to focus on the architectural requirements for a parallel machine. Finding the shortest length path between two vertices in a large graph serves as the example. The algorithm is appropriate because, besides being simple and useful, it is similar in character to the many "spreading activation" computations in artificial intelligence. The problem to be solved is this:

> Given a graph with vertices V and edges $E \subset V \times V$, with an arbitrary pair of vertices $a, b \in V$, find the length k of the shortest sequence of connected vertices $a, v_1, v_2, \dots b$ such that all the edges $(a, v_1), (v_1, v_2), \dots (v_k - 1, b) \in E$ are in the graph.

For concreteness, consider a graph with 10^4 vertices and an average of 10^2 randomly connected edges per vertex. (For examples of where such graphs might arise, see Quillian (1968), Collins and Loftus (1975), Waltz and Pollack (1985). In such a graph, almost any randomly chosen pair of vertices will be connected by a path of not more than three edges.

The algorithm for finding the shortest path from vertex A to vertex B begins by labeling every vertex with its distance from A. This is accomplished by labeling vertex A with 0, labeling all vertices connected to A with 1, labeling all unlabeled vertices connected to those vertices with 2, and so on. (See figure 1.5.) The process terminates as soon as vertex B is labeled. The label of B is then the length of the shortest connecting path. Any path with monotonically decreasing labels originating from B will lead to A in this number of steps. A common optimization of this algorithm is to propagate the labels from A and B simultaneously until they meet, but for the sake of clarity I will stick to its simplest form.

Ideally, we should be able to describe the algorithm to the computer as something like this:

Algorithm I: "Finding the length of shortest path from A to B"

1. Label all vertices with $+\infty$.

2. Label vertex A with 0.

3. Label every vertex, except A, with 1 plus the minimum of its neighbor's labels and itself. Repeat this step until the label of vertex B is finite.

4. Terminate. The label of B is the answer.

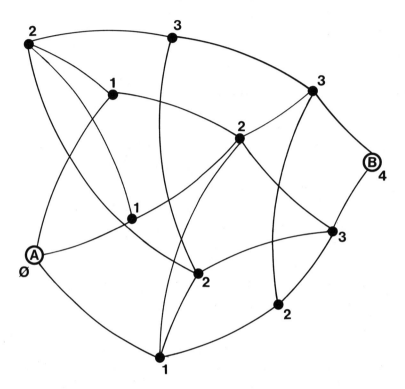

Figure 1.5 Algorithm I finds the length of the shortest path from vertex A to vertex B by labeling each point with its distance from A.

I use this example of a path-length algorithm to motivate the structure of the Connection Machine.

Algorithms of this type are slow on a conventional computer. Assuming that each step written above takes unit time, Algorithm I will terminate in a time proportional to the length of the connecting path. For the 10^4 vertex random graph mentioned above, Step 3 will be repeated two or three times, so about six steps will be required to find the path length. Unfortunately, the steps given above do not correspond well with the kinds of steps that can be executed on a von Neumann machine. Direct translation of the algorithm into Lisp gives this an inefficient program. The program runs in a time proportional to the number of vertices times the length of the path times the average degree of each vertex. For example, the graph mentioned above would require several million executions of the inner loop. Finding a path in a test graph required about an hour of CPU time on a VAX-11/750 Computer.

Besides being slow, a serial program implements dissimilar operations with similar constructs, resulting in a more obscure rendition of the original algorithm. For example, in the algorithm, iteration is used only to specify multiple operations that need to take place in time-sequential order, which is where the sequencing is critical to the algorithm. In a serial program everything must take place in sequence. The iteration would be used not only to do things that are rightfully sequential but also to operate all the elements of a set and to find the minimum of a set of numbers.

A good programmer could, of course, change the algorithm to one that would run faster. For example, it is not necessary to propagate labels from every labeled vertex but only from those that have just changed. There are also many well-studied optimizations for particular types of graphs. We have become so accustomed to making such modifications that we tend to make them without even noticing. Most programmers, given the task of implementing Algorithm I, probably would include several such optimizations almost automatically. Of course, many "optimizations" would help some graphs and hurt others. For instance, in a fully connected graph the extra overhead of checking if a vertex has just changed would slow things down. Also, with optimizations it becomes more difficult to understand what is going on. Optimization trades speed for clarity and flexibility.

Instead of optimizing the algorithm to match the operation of the von Neumann machine, we could make a machine to match the algorithm. Implementing Algorithm I directly will lead us to the architecture of the Connection Machine.

Requirement I: Many Processors

To implement the path-length algorithm directly, we need concurrency. As Algorithm I is described, there are steps when all the vertices change to a computed value simultaneously. To make these changes all at once, there must be a processing element associated with each vertex. Because the graph can have an arbitrarily large number of vertices, the machine needs an arbitrarily large number of processing elements. Unfortunately, although it is fine to demand infinite resources, any physical machine will be only finite. What compromise should we be willing to make?

It would suffice to have a machine with enough processors to deal with most of the problems that arise. How big a machine this is depends on the problems. It will be a trade-off between cost and functionality.

We are already accustomed to making this kind of trade-off for the amount of memory on a computer. Any real memory is finite, but it is practical to make the memory large enough so that our models of the machine can safely ignore the limitations. We should be willing to accept similar limitations on the number of processors. Of course, as with memory, there will always be applications in which we have to face the fact of finiteness. In a von Neumann machine we generally assume that the memory is large enough to hold the data to be operated on, plus a reasonable amount of working storage, say, in proportion to the size of the problem. For the shortest path problem we will make similar assumptions about the availability of processors. This will be the first design requirement for the machine: that there be enough processing elements to be allocated as needed, in proportion to the size of the problem.

A corollary of this requirement is that each processing element must be as small and as simple as possible so that we can afford to have as many of them as we want. In particular, a processing element can have only a small amount of memory. This is an important design constraint. It limits what we can expect to do within a single processing element. It would not be reasonable to assume both "there are plenty of processors" and "there is plenty of memory per processor." If the machine is to be built, it must use roughly the same number of components as conventional machines. Modern production technology gives us one "infinity" by allowing inexpensive replication of components. It is not fair to ask for two.

Requirement II: Programmable Connections

In the path-length algorithm, the pattern of interelement communication depends on the structure of the graph. The machine must work for arbitrary graphs, so every processing element must have the potential of communicating with every other processing element. The pattern of connections must be a part of the changeable state of the machine. (In other problems we actually want to change the connections dynamically during the course of the computation, but this is not necessary for the path-length calculation.)

From the standpoint of the software the connections must be programmable, but the processors may have a fixed *physical* wiring scheme. Here again there is an analogy with memory. In a conventional computer the storage elements for memory locations 4 and 5 are located in close physical proximity, whereas location 1000 may be physically on the other side of the machine, but to the software they are all equally easy to access. If the machine has virtual memory, location 1000 may be on a disk and may require much more time to access. From the software this is invisible. It is no more difficult to move an item from location 4 to 1000 than it is from 4 to 5. We would like a machine that hides the physical connectivity of the processors as thoroughly as the von Neumann computer hides the physical locality of its memory. This is an important part of molding the structure of our machine to the structure of the problem. It forms the second requirement for the machine: that the processing elements be connected by software.

This ability to configure the topology of the machine to match the topology of the problem turns out to be one of the most important features of the Connection Machine. (That is why it is called a Connection Machine.) It is also the feature that presents the greatest technical difficulties. To visualize how such a communications network works, imagine that each processing element is connected to its own message *router* and that the message routers are arranged like the crosspoints of a grid, each physically connected to its

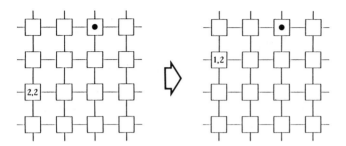

Figure 1.6 A simple (but inefficient) communications network topology.

four immediate neighbors (figure 1.6). Assume that one processing element needs to communicate with another one, say, 2 up and 3 to the right. It passes a message to its router, which contains the information to be transmitted plus a label specifying that it is to be sent 2 up and 3 over. On the basis of that label, the router sends the message to its neighbor on the right, modifying the label to say "2 up and 2 over." That processor then forwards the message again, and so on, until the label reads "0 up and 0 over." At that point the router receiving the message delivers it to the connected processing element.

In practice, a grid is not really a good way to connect the routers because routers can be separated by as many as $2\sqrt{n}$ intermediaries. It is desirable to use much more complicated physical connection schemes with lots of shortcuts so that the maximum distance between any two cells is small. We also need to select the routing algorithms carefully to avoid "traffic jams" when many messages are traveling through the network at once. These problems are discussed in detail in chapter 4. The important thing here is that processing elements communicate by sending messages through routers. Only the routers need worry about the physical connection topology. So long as two processing elements know each other's addresses, they can communicate as if they were physically connected. We say that there is a *virtual connection* between them. The virtual connection presents a consistent interface between processors. Since the implementation details are invisible, the software can remain the same as technology changes, wires break, and hardware designers think of new tricks.

In the path-length algorithm, a vertex must communicate with all its neighbors. The *fanout* of the communication is equal to the number of neighbors of the vertex. Since a vertex can have an arbitrary number of connected edges, the fanout of a processing element must be unlimited. Similarly, a vertex can receive communication from an arbitrarily large number of edges simultaneously; a processing element must be able to send to and receive from an arbitrary number of others.

Does this mean that each processing element must be large enough to handle many messages at once? Will it need arbitrary amounts of storage to remember all its connections? Providing large amounts of storage contradicts the need to keep the processing elements small. Fortunately there is a better method: *fanout trees*.

Trees Allow Arbitrary Fanout

The term "fanout tree" comes from electrical engineering. A related fanout problem comes up electrically because it is impossible to measure a signal without disturbing it. This sounds like a mere principle of physics, but every engineer knows its macroscopic consequences. In standard digital electronics, for instance, no gate can directly drive more than about ten others. If it is necessary to drive more than this, then it can be accomplished by a tree of buffers. One gate drives ten buffers, each of which drive ten more, and so on, until the desired fanout is achieved. This is called a fanout tree.

There is a software equivalent to this in languages such as Lisp, where large data structures are built out of small, fixed-size components. The Lisp "cons cell" has room for only two pointers. Sequences of arbitrary many elements are represented by stringing together multiple cons cells. Lisp programmers use linear lists more often than trees because they are better suited to sequential access. Balanced trees are used when the time to access an arbitrary element is important.

The use of trees to represent a network with fanout is illustrated in figure 1.7. Notice that each node is connected to no more than three others. (Lisp gets away with two because the connections are not bidirectional, so it does not store the "backpointers.") Because a balanced tree with N leaves requires $2N - 1$ nodes, the number of 3-connected processing elements required to represent any graph is equal to twice the number of edges minus the number of vertices. The tree structure "wastes" memory by storing the internal structure of the tree, just as the Lisp list "wastes" a factor of two in storage by storing the links from one node to the next. But because each vertex of the graph is represented by a tree of processing elements rather than by a single processing element, there is storage and processing power at each vertex in proportion to the number of connected edges. This solves the problem of how to handle multiple messages arriving at once. Each processing element only needs to handle a maximum of three messages. It also keeps the size of the elements small since each needs only the addresses that correspond to three virtual connections. There is a cost in time: A vertex must communicate data through its internal tree before the data can be communicated to the connected vertices. This internal communication requires $O(\log V)$ message transmission steps, where V is the degree of the vertex.

1.5   The Connection Machine Architecture

In the preceding sections I have identified two requirements for a machine to solve the path-length problem:

- Requirement I: There are enough processing elements to be allocated as needed, in proportion to the size of the problem.

- Requirement II: The processing elements can be connected by software.

The Connection Machine architecture follows directly from these two requirements. It provides a large number of tiny processor/memory cells connected by a programmable communications network. Each cell is sufficiently small so that it is incapable of performing meaningful computation on its own. Instead, multiple cells are connected together into data-dependent patterns, called *active data structures*, that both represent and process the data. The activities of these active data structures are directed from outside the Connection Machine by a conventional *host* computer. This host computer stores data structures on the Connection Machine in much the same

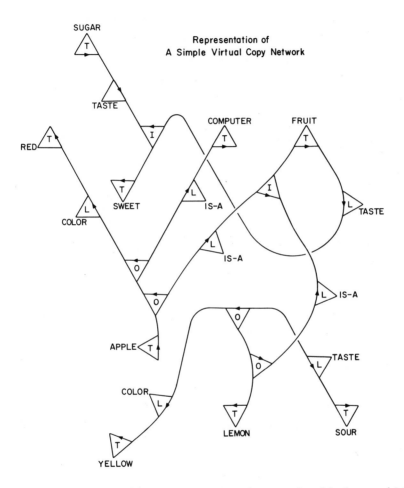

Figure 1.7   Use of trees to represent a network with fanout (this is the representation of the semantic network shown in Figure 1.4).

way that a conventional machine stores them in a memory. Unlike a conventional memory, though, the Connection Machine has no processor/memory bottleneck. The memory cells themselves do the processing. More precisely, the computation takes place through the coordinated interaction of the cells in the data structure. Because thousands or even millions of processing cells work on the problem simultaneously, the computation proceeds much more rapidly than would be possible on a conventional machine.

A Connection Machine is connected to a conventional computer much like a conventional memory. Its internal state can be read and written a word at a time from the conventional machine. It differs from a conventional memory in three respects. First, associated with each cell of storage is a processing cell that can perform local computations based on the information stored in that cell. Second, there exists a general intercommunications network that can connect all the cells in an arbitrary pattern. Third, there is a high-bandwidth input/output channel that can transfer data between the Connection Machine and peripheral devices at a much higher rate than would be possible through the host.

A *connection* is formed between two processing memory cells by storing a pointer in the memory. These connections can be set up by the host, loaded through the input/output channel, or determined dynamically by the Connection Machine itself.

In the prototype machine described in chapter 4, there are 65,536 processor/memory cells, each with 4,096 bits of memory. This is a small Connection Machine. The block diagram of the Connection Machine with hosts, processor/memory cells, communications network, and input/output is shown in figure 1.8.

The control of the individual processor/memory cells is orchestrated by the host of the computer. For example, the host may ask each cell that is in a certain state to add two of its memory locations locally and pass the resulting sum to a connected cell through the communications network. Thus a single command from the host can result in tens of thousands of additions and a permutation of data that depends on the pattern of connections. Each processor/memory cell is so small that it is essentially incapable of computing or even storing any significant computation on its own. Instead, computation takes place in the orchestrated interaction of thousands of cells through the

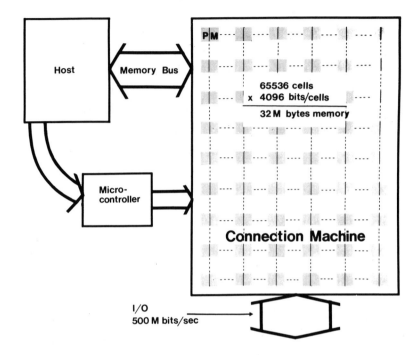

Figure 1.8 Block diagram of the CM-1 prototype Connection Machine.

communications network.

1.6   Issues in Designing Parallel Machines

The remainder of this book is devoted primarily to the dual questions of
how to use the architecture to solve problems and how to implement the
architecture in terms of available technology. In other words, how do we
program it and how do we build it? First, we must establish that we are
programming and building the right thing. Parallel processing is inevitable,
but what form will it take? So little is known about parallel computation that
informed, intelligent architects make different decisions when confronted with
the same set of choices. In this section I outline three of the most important
choices in designing any parallel machine:

- general versus fixed communication,

- fine versus coarse granularity, and

- multiple versus single instruction streams.

Although each issue can be characterized by the extreme schools of thought,
each offers a spectrum of choices rather than a binary decision. Each choice
is relatively independent, so in principle there is a different type of computer
architecture for each combination of choices.

General versus Fixed Communication

Some portion of the computation in all parallel machines involves communication among the individual processing elements. In some machines, such
communication is allowed in only a few specific patterns defined by the hardware. For example, the processors may be arranged in a two-dimensional grid
with each processor connected to its north, south, east, and west neighbors.
A single operation on such a machine sends a number from each processor to
its northern neighbor. Proposed connection patterns for such fixed-topology
machines include rings, n-dimensional cubes, and binary trees. The alternative to a fixed topology is a general communications network that permits
any processor to communicate with any other. An extreme example of an
architecture with such a general communications scheme is the hypothetical

paracomputer (Schwartz 1980b), in which every processor can simultaneously access a common shared memory. In a paracomputer, any two processors can communicate by referencing the same memory location.

Depending on how a general communications network is implemented, some pairs of processors may be able to communicate more quickly than others, because even in general communications schemes the network has an underlying unchanging physical pattern of wires and cables that can be visible to the programmer in different degrees. At the other extreme, a fixed-topology machine can be programmed to emulate a general machine with varying difficulty and efficiency.

The primary advantage of fixed-topology machines is simplicity. For problems in which the hardwired pattern is well matched to the application, fixed-topology machines can be faster. Examples of such matches are the use of a two-dimensional grid pattern for image processing and a shuffle-exchange pattern for Fast Fourier Transforms. The general communications machines have the potential of being fast and easier to program for a wider range of problems, particularly those that have less structured patterns of communication. Another potential advantage is that the connection pattern can change dynamically to optimize for particular data sets or to bypass faulty components.

Fine Grained versus Coarse Grained

In any parallel computer with multiple processing elements, there is a trade-off between the number and the size of the processors. The conservative approach uses as few as possible of the largest available processors. The conventional, single-processor von Neumann machine is the extreme case of this. The opposite approach achieves as much parallelism as possible by using a large number of small machines. We can characterize machines with tens or hundreds of relatively large processors as coarse grained and machines with tens of thousands to millions of small processors as fine grained. There are also many intermediate possibilities.

The fine grained processors have the potential of being faster because of the larger degree of parallelism. But more parallelism does not necessarily mean greater speed. The individual processors in the small-grained design are necessarily less powerful, so many small processors may be slower than one large one. For almost any application there are at least some portions of the code that run most efficiently on a single processor. For this reason, fine grained architectures are usually designed to be used in conjunction with a conventional single-processor host computer.

Perhaps the most important issue here is one of programming style. Since serial processor machines are coarse grained, the technology for programming coarse grained machines is better understood. It is plausible to expect a Fortran compiler to optimize code for, say, sixteen processing units, but not for sixteen thousand. On the other hand, if the algorithm is written with parallel processing in mind from the start, it may be that it divides naturally into the processors of a fine-grained machine. For example, in a vision application it may be most natural to specify a local algorithm to be performed on each point in an image, so a 1000×1000 point image would most naturally fit onto a million processor machine.

Multiple versus Single Instruction Streams

A Multiple Instruction Multiple Data (MIMD) machine is a collection of connected autonomous computers, each capable of executing its own program. Usually a MIMD machine also includes mechanisms for synchronizing operations between processors when desired. In a Single Instruction Multiple Data (SIMD) machine, all processors are controlled from a single instruction stream that is broadcast to all the processing elements simultaneously. Each processor typically has the option of executing an instruction or ignoring it, depending on the processor's internal state. Thus, although every processing element does not necessarily execute the same sequence of instructions, each processor is presented with the same sequence. Processors not executing must "wait out" while the active processors execute.

Although SIMD machines have only one instruction stream, they differ from MIMD machines by no more that a multiplicative constant in speed. A SIMD machine can simulate a MIMD machine in linear time by executing an interpreter, which interprets each processor's data as instructions. Similarly, a MIMD machine can simulate a SIMD. Such a simulation of a MIMD machine with a SIMD machine (or vice versa) may or may not be a desirable thing to do, but the possibility at least reduces the question from one of philosophy to one of engineering: Because both types of machines can do the same thing, which can do it faster or with less hardware?

The correct choice depends on the application. For well-structured problems with regular patterns of control, SIMD machines have the edge, because more of the hardware is devoted to operations on the data. This is because the SIMD machine, with only one instruction stream, can share most of its control hardware among all processors. In applications in which the control flow required of each processing element is complex and data dependent, MIMD architecture has the advantage. The shared instruction stream can follow only one branch of the code at a time, so each possible branch must be executed in sequence, whereas the uninterested processor is idle. The result is that processors in a SIMD machine may sit idle much of the time.

The other issue in choosing between a SIMD and a MIMD architecture is one of programmability. Here there are arguments on both sides. The SIMD machine eliminates problems of synchronization. On the other hand, it does so by taking away the possibility of operating asynchronously. Because either type of machine can efficiently emulate the other, it is desirable to choose one style for programming and the other for hardware.

Gordon Bell (1985) characterized SIMD and MIMD machines as having different characteristic "synchronization times" and pointed out that different MIMD machines have different characteristic times between processor synchronization steps that vary from every few instructions to entire tasks. There are also SIMD machines that allow varying amounts of autonomy for the individual processing elements and/or several instruction streams, so once again this issue presents a spectrum of possible choices.

1.7   Comparison with Other Architectures

Different architectures make different choices with respect to the key decisions outlined in the previous section. In this section I contrast the Connection Machine architecture with some other approaches to building high performance computers. The most important distinguishing feature of the Connection Machine is the combination of fine granularity and general communication. The Connection Machine has a large number of small processors. This provides a high degree of parallelism and helps solve resource-allocation problems. Also, the communications network allows the connectivity of these processors to be reconfigured to match a problem. This ability to "wire up" thousands of programmable processing units is really the heart of the Connection Machine concept. In what follows I summarize some of the approaches taken by other architectures. For references to specific examples see the notes at the end of this chapter.

Fast von Neumann Machines

There are a large number of ongoing efforts to push the performance of conventional serial machines. These involve the use of faster switching devices, the use of larger and more powerful instruction sets, the use of smaller and simpler instruction sets, improvements in packaging, and tailoring the machines to specific applications. Even if the most exotic of these projects were completely successful, they would not come close to meeting our performance requirements. When performing simple computations on large amounts of data, von Neumann computers are limited by the bandwidth between memory and processor. This is a fundamental flaw in the von Neumann design; it cannot be eliminated by clever engineering.

Networks of Conventional Machines

Other researchers have proposed connecting dozens or even hundreds of conventional computers by shared memory or a high bandwidth communications network. Several of these architectures are good candidates for machines with orders of magnitude of increased performance. Compared with the Connection Machine, these architectures have a relatively small number of relatively large machines. These machines have a much lower ratio of processing power to memory size, so they are fundamentally slower than the Connection Machine on memory intensive operations.

Machines with Fixed Topologies

Much closer to the Connection Machine in the degree of potential parallelism are the tessellated or recursive structures of many small machines. The most common topologies are the two-dimensional grid or torus. These machines have fixed interconnection topologies, and their programs are written to take advantage of the topology. When the structure of the problem matches the structure of the machine, these architectures can exhibit the same or a higher degree of concurrency as the Connection Machine. Unlike the Connection Machine, their topologies cannot be reconfigured to match a particular problem. This is particularly important in problems such as logic simulation and semantic network inference, for which the topology is highly irregular.

Database Processors

There have been several special-purpose architectures proposed for speeding up database search operations. Like the Connection Machine, these database processors are designed to perform data-intensive operations under control of a more conventional host computer. Although these machines are designed to process a restricted class of queries on larger databases, they have many implementation issues in common with the Connection Machine. The study of these architectures has produced a significant body of theory on the computational complexity of parallel database operations.

Marker Propagation Machines

The Connection Machine architecture was originally developed to implement the marker-propagation programs for retrieving data from semantic networks (Fahlman 1979). The Connection Machine is well suited for executing marker-type algorithms, but it is considerably more flexible than special-purpose marker propagators. The Connection Machine has a computer at each node that can manipulate address pointers and send arbitrary messages. It is capable of building structures dynamically. These features are important for applications other than marker-passing.

Cellular Automata and Systolic Arrays

A systolic array is a tessellated structure of synchronous cells that perform fixed sequences of computations with fixed patterns of communication. By contrast, in the Connection Machine both computations and the communications patterns are programmable. In the Connection Machine, uniformity is not critical. Some cells can be defective or missing. Another structure, similar to the systolic array, is cellular automata. In an abstract sense, the Connection Machine is a universal cellular automaton with an additional mechanism added for nonlocal communication. In other words, the Connection Machine hardware hides the details. This additional mechanism makes a large difference in performance and ease of programming.

Content Addressable Memories

The Connection Machine can be used as a content addressable or associative memory, but it is also able to perform nonlocal computations through the communications network. The elements in content addressable memories are comparable in size with connection memory cells, but they are not generally programmable. When used as a content addressable memory, the Connection Machine processors allow more complex matching procedures.

1.8   The Rest of the Story

In the remainder of this book I discuss in detail how to program and build Connection Machines. In chapter 2 I describe a programming language based on Lisp that provides an idealized model of what a Connection Machine should do in the same sense that a conventional programming language provides an idealized model of a conventional machine. In chapter 3 I discuss some of the issues that arise in implementing the architecture and hardware. The details of an actual prototype are described in chapter 4, and active data structures and a description of some of the fundamental algorithms for the Connection Machine are discussed in chapter 5. In chapter 6, on storage allocation, I show how these data structures can be built and transformed dynamically. It also discusses the related issue of why a Connection Machine can work even when some of its components do not. The final chapter, chapter 7, is a philosophical discussion of computer architecture and what the science of computation may look like in the future.

Most of the references to related works have been moved out of the text and into the notes at the end of each chapter. There is also an annotated bibliography at the end of the document that gives for each reference some justification of why it might be worth reading in this context.

1.9 Notes

The quest to make a thinking machine is not new. The first reference of which I am aware in the literature is *Politics*, in which Aristotle writes of autonomous machines that can understand the needs of their masters as an alternative to slavery. For centuries this remained only a dream, until the 1940s, when an increased understanding of servomechanisms led to the establishment of the field of *cybernetics* (Wiener 1948, Ashby 1956). Cybernetic systems were largely analog. Soon afterward, the development of digital computing machinery gave rise to comparisons with the symbolic functions of the mind (Turing 1950, von Neumann 1945), which led in the early 1960s to the development of the field of *artificial intelligence* (Minsky 1961, Newell and Simon 1963). For a readable history of these developments, see Boden (1977).

For insight to the motivation of the two-part von Neumann design (including some amusing predictions of things like potential applications and memory sizes), I suggest reading some of the original documents (Burks 1946, 1957, Goldstine and von Neumann 1948, von Neumann 1945). For a good, brief introduction to semantic networks, see Woods (1975). For examples of specific semantic network representation schemes, see Brachman (1978a and 1978b), Fahlman (1979), Hewitt, Attardi, and Simi (1980), Shapiro (1976), and Szolovitz et al. (1977), and in particular for semantic networks designed to be accessed by parallel algorithms, see Quillian (1968), Fahlman (1979), and Woods (1978). For discussions of the semantics of semantic networks, see Brachman (1978), Hendrix (1975), and Woods (1975). There are many other knowledge representation schemes in artificial intelligence that were designed with parallelism in mind, for example, "connectionist" theories (Feldman and Ballard (1981), *k*-lines (Minsky 1979), word-expert parsing (Small 1980), massively parallel parsing (Waltz and Pollack 1985), schema mechanisms (Drescher 1985), and classifier systems (Holland 1959). It may also be that parallelism is applicable to the access of the highly structured knowledge in expert systems (Stefik et al. 1982). One of the most exciting potential application areas of the machine is in systems that actually learn from experience. Such applications would be able to use to advantage the Connection Machine's ability to dynamically change its own connections.

For examples of recent approaches to learning, see Winston (1980), Hopfield (1982), and Minsky (1982).

For a recent survey of parallel computing, see Haynes et al. (1982) and Bell (1985). My discussion of the issues in this chapter follows the taxonomy introduced in Schwartz (1983). For a fun-to-read paper on the need for raw power and parallelism, see Moravec (1979). The phrase "von Neumann bottleneck" comes from Backus's Turing Lecture (Backus 1978), in which he eloquently sounds the battle cry against word-at-a-time thought.

For examples of alternative parallel architectures the reader is referred to the annotated bibliography at the end of the book. The references therein can be divided as follows. Large- to medium-grain machines: Bell (1985), Bouknight (1972), Buehrer et al. (1982), Chakravarthy et al. (1982), Davidson (1980), Gajski et al. (1983b), Gottlieb and coworkers (1982, 1983) Halstead (1979, 1980), Hewitt (1980), Keller et al. (1978, 1979), Kuck and Stokes (1982), Lundstrom and Barnes (1980), Rieger and coworkers (1979, 1980), Schwartz (1980a, 1980b), Shin et al. (1982), Slotnick et al. (1978), Stolfo and Shaw (1982), Sullivan and Bashkow (1977), Swan et al. (1977), Treleaven and Moll (1980), Trujillo (1982), Ward (1978), and Widdoes (1980). Small-grain machines: Batcher (1974, 1980), Browning (1980), Carroll (1980), DiGiacinto (1981), Fahlman (1981), Gilmore (1982), Gritton et al. (1977), Holland (1959, 1960) Lee (1962), Mago (1979), Schaefer (1982), Shaw (1982), Snyder (1982), and Surprise (1981). Database machines: Copeland (1973), Hawthorn and DeWitt (1982), Kung (1980), and Ozkarahan et al. (1974). Data flow: Arvind and coworkers (1978, 1983), and Dennis and coworkers (1977, 1980). Special purpose machines: Chang (1978), Forster (1982), Hawkins, (1963) Kung (1980), Lipovski (1978), Meadows (1974), Parhami (1972), Reeves (1981), and Siegel et al. (1981). Content addressable memories: Lee (1962) and Lee and Paul (1963).

For some comparisons of the performance of various machines, see Dongarra (1984), Tenenbaum (1983), and Hawthorn and DeWitt (1982). Not all computations can be speeded up by parallel processing. For an example beyond help, see Hillis (1983).

Chapter 2

How to Program a Connection Machine

2.1 Connection Machine Lisp Models the Connection Machine

It is easy to forget how closely conventional languages correspond to the hardware of a conventional computer, even for "high-level" languages like Lisp. The control flow in Lisp, for example, is essentially an abstract version of the hardware instruction fetching mechanism of a serial machine. Objects are pointers. CAR and CDR are indirect addresses. Function invocation is a subroutine call. Assignment is storing in memory. This close correspondence between Lisp and the machine on which it is implemented accounts for much of the language's power and popularity. It makes it easy to write compilers. It makes the language easier to think about and, more important, it allows the performance of algorithms to be compared and estimated without reference to the details of a particular machine. The language captures what is common and essential to a wide range of serial computers while hiding the details that set them apart.

Connection Machine Lisp (CmLisp) is an extension of Common Lisp, designed to support the parallel operations of the Connection Machine. It is intended to be for the Connection Machine architecture what Lisp is for the serial computer: an expression of the essential character of the architecture that leaves out the details of implementation. In the sense that Fortran or Lisp are abstract versions of a conventional computer, CmLisp is an abstract version of the Connection Machine. Just as these languages hide such details of the computer as word length, instruction set, and low-level storage conventions, CmLisp hides the details of the Connection Machine. Just as conventional languages reflect the architecture of conventional computers, CmLisp reflects the architecture of the Connection Machine. The structure of the language follows the structure of the hardware.

An example of this correspondence is the relatively conventional control structure of CmLisp, which is similar to languages such as FP and APL. In CmLisp, as in the Connection Machine itself, parallelism is achieved through simultaneous operations over composite data structures rather than through concurrent control structures. In this sense CmLisp is a relatively conservative parallel language, because it retains the program flow and control constructs of a normal serial Lisp but allows operations to be performed simultaneously across each element of a large data structure. This mirrors the hardware of the Connection Machine, where the top level control is orchestrated by a conventional serial computer with thousands of values simultaneously calculated by the individual processor/memory cells.

Why Lisp?

Lisp was chosen as a base for developing a Connection Machine language for a combination of technical and social reasons. On the technical side, Lisp is extensible, has dynamic storage allocation, and is generally good for symbol manipulation. In addition, excellent Lisp programming environments already exist. On the sociological side, most members of the artificial intelligence community, for whom the Connection Machine was originally designed, are already familiar with Lisp. The supporting infrastructure for their environments — documentation, primers, software libraries and programming cliches — have taken years to develop and years to learn, so it makes sense to build onto what already exists.

Most of the ideas in the language are actually relatively independent of Lisp and would be equally applicable to Connection Machine versions of Algol, C, or even Fortran.

In this chapter I describe CmLisp. It is an introduction to the language, intended for readers who are already familiar with ordinary Lisp. It is not a programming manual. For a more detailed specification of the language, see *The Connection Machine Lisp Manual* (Hillis and Steele (1985)).

Xectors

All concurrent operations in CmLisp involve a simple data structure called a *xector* (pronounced zek′tor). A xector corresponds roughly to a set of processors with a value stored in each processor. Because a xector is distributed across many processors, it is possible to operate on all its elements simultaneously. To add two xectors together, for example, the Connection Machine directs each processor to add the corresponding values locally, producing a third xector of the sums. This requires only a single addition time, even though the xector may have hundreds of thousands of elements.

CmLisp supports many potentially concurrent operations to combine, create, modify, and reduce xectors. These operations could be implemented on a conventional computer, but they would be much slower, perhaps tens of thousands of times slower, than they are on the Connection Machine. CmLisp also allows the programmer to define new xector operations that execute concurrently. This is the source of its power.

It would be inelegant to force the CmLisp programmer to think in terms of processors and memory locations. The xector data structure provides a cleaner abstraction that can be simply translated into these machine-dependent concepts. Each xector is defined by three components: a *domain*, a *range*, and a *mapping* between them. The domain and range are sets of Lisp objects, and the mapping assigns a single object in the range to each object of the domain. Each object in the domain is called an *index* of the xector. Each object in the range is called a *value*. An index/value pair is called an *element*. In mathematical terms, a xector is a set of elements with unique indices or, equivalently, a function from Lisp objects to Lisp objects.

On a serial machine a xector can be implemented as some kind of lookup table with each index used as a key to find its corresponding value. In the Connection Machine each element of the xector is stored in a separate processor, and the index is the name of the processor, an address in the memory of the host machine. A programmer does not really need to know this, but it helps in visualizing how it works.

Xector Notation

To write a xector I list the elements surrounded by set braces. For each element I show the index and value, connected by an arrow. For example, the following expression denotes a xector that maps the symbols SKY, GRASS, APPLE onto the symbols BLUE, GREEN, RED, respectively:

   {SKY→BLUE GRASS→GREEN   APPLE→RED}

This is the most general form of a xector. There are also some important special cases that deserve their own refinements of the notation.

One such special type xector is one in which each index maps onto itself. This is used to represent a *set*, namely, the set of indices. When the index and the value are the same, we can omit the arrow and write the value only once (the symbol ≡ denotes equivalence):

   {A→A   1→1   2→2} ≡ {A   1   2}

Another important special case is when the domain of the xector is a sequence of integers starting from zero. In this case we use a bracket notation suggestive of a vector:

   {0→A   1→B   2→C   →D} ≡ [A   B   C   D]

The final special case is a *constant* xector which maps every possible index into a single value. In this case the value is written only once, with the index left unspecified:

   {→3}

This denotes the constant xector that maps every object onto the number three.

All these notational conventions are recognized by the CmLisp reader and generated by the CmLisp printer.

Creating, Referencing, and Modifying Xectors

Xectors are normal Lisp objects. They can be printed, bound to variables, stored in arrays, returned from functions, and so on, just as one would expect with any first-class Lisp object.

The easiest way to create a xector is to type it explicitly to the reader (the symbol ⇒ denotes evaluation):

```
(SETQ COLOR-OF '{SKY→BLUE   APPLE→RED   GRASS→GREEN})
⇒ {APPLE→RED   GRASS→GREEN   SKY→BLUE}
```

The expression above sets the value of the symbol `COLOR-OF` to the example xector. Notice that when the xector is printed the elements are shown in a different order. CmLisp will always reorder the elements of a xector according to a *canonical ordering* of the indices. This ordering is the same for all xectors. Integer indices are always in monotonically increasing order, but otherwise the canonical ordering is unspecified and may vary from implementation to implementation.

The values of a xector can be referenced by the function `XREF`, which finds the value of a xector corresponding to a given index. If the index is not specified by the xector, `XREF` will signal an error. For example,

```
(XREF COLOR-OF 'APPLE) ⇒ RED
```

```
(XREF COLOR-OF 'COW)   ⇒ error
```

Similarly, the values of a xector can be changed with the `XSET` function:

```
(XSET 'BLUE COLOR-OF 'GRASS)
```

```
COLOR-OF ⇒ {APPLE→RED   GRASS→BLUE   SKY→BLUE}
```

`XSET` also signals an error if the index is out of range, but the function `XMOD` adds a new index/value pair if necessary:

```
(XMOD 'GREEN COLOR-OF 'GRASS)
⇒ {APPLE→RED   GRASS→GREEN   SKY→BLUE}
```

```
(XMOD 3 '{ONE→1   TWO→2} 'THREE)
⇒ {ONE→1   TWO→2   THREE→3}
```

Because xectors represent functions, CmLisp uses some of the terminology of functions to refer to their parts and properties. The set of indices over which a xector is defined is called the *domain*. The set of values into which it maps is called the *range*. If all the values are unique, then the xector is *invertible*, in which case the *inverse* is the xector that maps each value back to its corresponding index:

```
(RANGE COLOR-OF)    ⇒ {RED   GREEN   BLUE}


(DOMAIN COLOR-OF)   ⇒ {APPLE   GRASS  SKY}


(INVERSE COLOR-OF)  ⇒ {RED→APPLE   GREEN→GRASS   BLUE→SKY}
```

Xectors can be created using conventional Lisp objects as templates. Similarly, Lisp objects can be created from xectors. The following functions are used to convert xectors on other data structures:

ALIST-TO-XECTOR	XECTOR-TO-ALIST
HASHTABLE-TO-XECTOR	XECTOR-TO-HASHTABLE
PLIST-TO-XECTOR	XECTOR-TO-PLIST
LISTS-TO-XECTOR	XECTOR-TO-LISTS
ARRAY-TO-XECTOR	XECTOR-TO-ARRAY
LIST-TO-XECTOR	XECTOR-TO-LIST
SEQUENCE-TO-XECTOR	XECTOR-TO-SEQUENCE

The last three pairs of functions convert ordered sequences to xectors. In these cases, the sequences are created with the values in the canonical order of the xector. The xectors are created with the zero-based sequence of integers as indices. Some examples are:

```
(xector-to-list '{A→x B→y})       ⇒ (x y)


(alist-to-xector '((A.x) (B.y)))  ⇒ {A→x B→y}


(list-to-xector '(A B C))         ⇒ [A B C]
```

There are also functions to produce a set, or *identity* xector, from lists, strings, or arrays.

Xectors as Sequences

Like a string or a list, a xector contains an ordered sequence of elements. Such an object is called a *sequence* in Common Lisp, and the language provides many generic functions that can operate on any type of sequence. In CmLisp these functions work on xectors also, using the canonical order of the indices as the order of the elements.

As illustrated in table 2.1, many of the generic sequence operations can execute more quickly on xectors than on lists or vectors. This is because the Connection Machine can operate on all the elements in a xector simultaneously. Operations such as SEARCH and DELETE, which can be performed on each element independently, execute in a fixed time no matter how many elements are in the xector. Operations that involve reducing, counting, or numbering the elements take place in logarithmic time, because they are implemented by algorithms on balanced trees. (Some of the operations listed in table 2.1 take an arbitrary Lisp function as one of the parameters. For the purpose of the table it is assumed that this function can be executed in unit time on both the host and the Connection Machine. The numbers reflect the assumption that communication and access of memory take place in unit time. A more accurate model would count both these times as logarithmic in the total size of the memory, for vectors, lists, and xectors.)

These "canned" operations are convenient, but they are not strictly necessary. All the functions in the table can be written in terms of lower-level parallel primitives. In the next section I show how.

2.2 Alpha Notation

In this section I introduce a way of describing the simple "all-at-once" parallelism that occurs in operations such as vector addition in which all elements can be processed independently. It is called *alpha notation*, and it requires extending the normal Lisp version of FUNCALL to a version that allows a xector of functions to be concurrently called on xectors of arguments. This is similar to Lisp *mapping* except that it is done in parallel.

In CmLisp the Greek letter *alpha* (α) is used to represent the conversion of a value into a constant xector, that is, into a xector that maps everything onto that value. In implementation terms, this is the equivalent of loading a

Table 2.1 Worst Case Running Times for Various Sequence Operations for Sequences of Length N.

Operation	Vector	List	Xector
ELT	0(1)	0(N)	0(1)
LENGTH	0(1)	0(N)	0(log N)
SUBSEQ	0(1)	0(N)	0(log N)
COPY-SEQ	0(N)	0(N)	0(1)
FILL	0(N)	0(N)	0(1)
REMOVE	0(N)	0(N)	0(1)
DELETE	0(N)	0(N)	0(1)
REPLACE	0(N)	0(N)	0(log N)
COUNT	0(N)	0(N)	0(log N)
REVERSE	0(N)	0(N)	0(log N)
POSITION	0(N)	0(N)	0(1)
REDUCE	0(N)	0(N)	0(log N)
SORT	0(N log N)	0(N log N)	$0(\log^2 N)$
MERGE	0(N)	0(N)	0(log N)
SEARCH	0(N)	0(N)	0(1)

value into every processor. When the symbol α precedes an expression, the expression is interpreted as a xector with the constant value of the expression. Some examples are:

$$\alpha 3 \qquad \Rightarrow \{\rightarrow 3\}$$
$$\alpha(+\ 1\ 2) \Rightarrow \{\rightarrow 3\}$$
$$\alpha+ \qquad \Rightarrow \{\rightarrow+\}$$

The last example is a xector of PLUS functions. A xector of functions has a special meaning when it occurs in the functional position of a CmLisp expression. When an expression is being evaluated, *a xector of functions is applied by concurrently mapping the xector across its arguments*; that is, each element of the function xector is applied to the values of argument elements with corresponding indices. The result returned is a xector of the individual results. For example,

$$(\alpha+\ '\{a{\rightarrow}1\ b{\rightarrow}2\}\ '\{a{\rightarrow}3\ b{\rightarrow}3\}) \qquad \Rightarrow \{a{\rightarrow}4\ b{\rightarrow}5\}$$

$$(\alpha\text{CONS}\ '\{a{\rightarrow}1\ b{\rightarrow}2\}\ '\{a{\rightarrow}3\ b{\rightarrow}3\}) \Rightarrow \{a{\rightarrow}(1\ .\ 3)\ b{\rightarrow}(2\ .\ 3)\}$$

Any index that does not occur in all elements is ignored:

$$(\alpha+\ '\{a{\rightarrow}1\ b{\rightarrow}2\ c{\rightarrow}3\}\ '\{a{\rightarrow}3\ b{\rightarrow}3\}) \Rightarrow \{a{\rightarrow}4\ b{\rightarrow}5\}$$

$$(\alpha\text{CONS}\ '\{a{\rightarrow}1\ b{\rightarrow}2\}\ \alpha 9) \qquad\qquad \Rightarrow\ '\{a{\rightarrow}(1\ .\ 9)\ b{\rightarrow}(2\ .\ 9)\}$$

Alpha notation has some useful algebraic properties. Notice that α can be factored outside an expression or it can be distributed across the components:

$$\alpha(+\ 1\ 2) \equiv (\alpha+\ \alpha 1\ \alpha 2)\,.$$

Both sides of the expressions immediately above evaluate the xector $\{\rightarrow 3\}$. The factored form of an alpha expression is generally more concise. This is especially true of more complex expressions with many nested subcomponents. Unfortunately, α can only be factored if every subexpression is multiplied by it. This is not normally the case.

Most CmLisp alpha expressions contain some subexpressions that evaluate xectors and do not need to be alpha converted. To allow the use of the factored form in this more general case, I introduce another symbol, •, that cancels the effect of α. Within an expression that is multiplied by α the dot can be placed in front of subexpressions that are not to be converted by α. The symbol has no meaning when it occurs outside such an expression that is multiplied by alpha. Some examples of how • works are (assume that x is bound to a xector):

α(+ •x 1) $\equiv$ (α+ x α1)

α(+ (* •x 2) 1) $\equiv$ (α+ (α* x α2) α1)

α •3 $\equiv$ 3

•3 $\Rightarrow$ *error*

By using dots, the programmer can specify different combinations of mapped and unmapped arguments to a function. For example, if A is the xector [A B C] and X is the xector [X Y Z], then:

(CONS A X) $\Rightarrow$ ([A B C] . [X Y Z])
α(CONS •A •X) $\Rightarrow$ [(A . X) (B . Y) (C . Z)]
α(CONS A •X) $\Rightarrow$ [([A B C] . X) ([A B C] . Y) ([A B C] . Z)]

One informal way to think of α is that it means "give me a zillion" of whatever is inside the expression, where a zillion is however many are needed. α produces a zillion additions, a zillion threes, or whatever. The dot symbol is a way of marking those subexpressions that already have a zillion.

The xector of functions in an alpha funcall does not necessarily have to be a constant xector. Different operations can be performed on different indexes:

(Funcall '[+ - - +] '[1 2 3 4] α1) $\Rightarrow$ [2 1 2 5]

Because this is implemented by different operations being performed in different processors, this use of xectors is related to the SIMD/MIMD distinctions in hardware discussed in chapter 1. On a MIMD machine, xector-mapped funcall of this sort is essentially a synchronization primitive because the different component functions take different amounts of time to execute. Full MIMD operation corresponds to αEVAL, applied to the xector of programs.

2.3 Beta Reduction

Alpha notation takes a single thing and makes many copies of it. Another common type of operation is to take many things and combine them into one. For this we use β, which converts a two-argument function into a function that reduces the elements of a xector into a single value. This reduction is performed in parallel in logarithmic time. Beta reduction uses only the values of the elements and ignores the indices. Some examples are:

$(\beta+$ '$\{$A$\rightarrow$1 B$\rightarrow$2 C$\rightarrow$3$\}) \Rightarrow$ 6

$(\beta$AND '[T T NIL T]) $\Rightarrow$ NIL

$(\beta$MAX $\{$1 3 5 7$\}) \Rightarrow$ 7

α and β can be combined to produce many useful functions:

(DEFUN XECTOR-LENGTH (x) $(\beta+$ α(PROG2 $\bullet x$ 1))
(DEFUN MAGNITUDE (x) (SQRT $(\beta+$ $(\alpha*$ x x))))
(DEFUN ALL-SAME $(x$ $y)$ $(\beta$AND $(\alpha=$ x y))

β can also be used with two arguments to construct a new xector from a given a range and domain:

$(\beta$ '$\{$A$\rightarrow$1 B$\rightarrow$2$\}$ '$\{$A$\rightarrow$X B$\rightarrow$Y$\}) \Rightarrow \{$X$\rightarrow$1 Y$\rightarrow$2$\}$

These uses of β may seem completely different, but they are really two special cases of a more general operation. This is explained in section 2.6.

2.4   Defining Data Structures with DEFSTRUCT (Background)

DEFSTRUCT is the Lisp mechanism for defining structures with named components. DEFSTRUCT is really a part of Common Lisp, not the CmLisp extension. It is described here because it is a relatively recent addition to Lisp, and it is important for programming the Connection Machine. The reader who is already familiar with DEFSTRUCT may wish to skip to the last paragraph of this section.

A *structure* is a composite object with named components. DEFSTRUCT is a mechanism for defining new types of structures. It allows the programmer to create effectively new datatypes with Lisp functions for accessing and modifying their components. Given the name of the type and the names of the components, DEFSTRUCT defines all these accessors automatically, along with a function for creating new instances of the structure.

As an example of how this works, assume that we are defining a new datatype called PIXEL to represent a dot on a color screen. Assume that each pixel has three components: RED-INTENSITY, GREEN-INTENSITY, and BLUE-INTENSITY.

```
(DEFSTRUCT (PIXEL)
    RED-INTENSITY
    GREEN-INTENSITY
    BLUE-INTENSITY)
```

Evaluation of this form defines four functions: MAKE-PIXEL, RED-INTENSITY, GREEN-INTENSITY, and BLUE-INTENSITY. The function MAKE-PIXEL creates and returns a new instance of a PIXEL structure each time it is invoked. For example, evaluating

```
(SETQ P (MAKE-PIXEL))
```

sets the value of P to a newly created PIXEL structure.

The functions RED-INTENSITY, GREEN-INTENSITY, and BLUE-INTENSITY are three accessor functions that are defined by DEFSTRUCT to access the components of any PIXEL structure. They can also be used to modify the object by means of SETF. For example, if P is a pixel, then

```
(RED-INTENSITY P)
```

returns the red intensity of P, and

```
(SETF (RED-INTENSITY P) 3)
```

modifies P so that its red intensity is three. This is demonstrated in the following sequence:

```
(SETQ P (MAKE-PIXEL))
(SETF (RED-INTENSITY P) 3)
(RED-INTENSITY P) ⇒ 3
```

DEFSTRUCT also defines various other useful functions, including PIXEL-P (for testing if a giver object is a PIXEL) and COPY-PIXEL (for creating a new PIXEL with the same components as an old one). These are only the basics. For a complete description of DEFSTRUCT and its many wonderful features, see *Common Lisp: The Language* (Steele 1984).

Connection Machine Lisp adds one additional feature to DEFSTRUCT. It provides a :CM option that allows the programmer to specify that all structures of a particular type are to be stored on the Connection Machine:

```
(DEFSTRUCT (PIXEL :CM)
    RED-INTENSITY
    GREEN-INTENSITY
    BLUE-INTENSITY)
```

This causes MAKE-PIXEL to store new pixel structures on the Connection Machine. The components of this Connection Machine pixel structure can be accessed and modified as before. The only difference is that each pixel structure is stored in its own processor/memory cell. This allows parallel xector operations to be performed on the structures or their components, for instance, the xector of all pixels or the xector of all red-nntensity.

2.5   An Example: The Path-Length Algorithm

We now have enough of the language defined to give a nontrivial example of CmLisp programming. I define, as an example, a function for finding the shortest path length between two vertices in a large graph, using the algorithm discussed in chapter 1.

Algorithm I used a simple breadth-first search, searching all possible paths in parallel. To find the shortest path from vertex A to vertex B, every vertex is labeled with its distance from A. This is accomplished by labeling vertex A with 0, labeling all vertices connected to A with 1, labeling all unlabeled vertices connected to those vertices with 2 and so on. The process terminates as soon as vertex B is labeled. The label of B is then the length of the shortest connecting path.

The informal description of Algorithm I is

Algorithm I: "Finding the length of shortest path from A to B"

1. Label all vertices with $+\infty$.

2. Label vertex A with 0.

3. Label every vertex, except A, with 1 plus the minimum of its neighbor's labels. Repeat this step until the label of vertex B is finite.

4. Terminate. The label of B is the answer.

The algorithm as expressed in CmLisp is the following (notice that there is one expression corresponding to each line in Algorithm I that finds the length of path from vertex A to vertex B in graph G):

```
(DEFUN PATH-LENGTH (A B G)
    α(SETF (LABEL •G) +INF)
    (SETF (LABEL A) 0)
    (LOOP UNTIL (< (LABEL B) +INF)
          DO α(SETF (LABEL •(REMOVE A G))
                    (1+ (βMIN α(LABEL •(NEIGHBORS •G))))))))
    (LABEL B))
```

To understand the program it is necessary to understand the representation used for the graph. The graph is represented as a set, specifically a set of vertices. Each vertex has two components: a label and a set of neighboring vertices. All these sets are represented by xectors. The vertices are represented by structures, which can be defined by the following expression:

```
(DEFSTRUCT (VERTEX :CM)
    LABEL
    NEIGHBORS)
```

The graph G that is passed to `PATH-LENGTH` is a xector of these vertex structures that have been set up in such a way that the `NEIGHBORS` of each vertex are some set of other vertices in the graph. In other words, the expression α(`NEIGHBORS` •`G`) evaluates a xector of xectors, representing the set of neighborhoods.

The first line of the program sets the label of every vertex in G to +INF, which is some large positive number. The next line sets the label of vertex A to zero. Notice that these first two lines have exactly the same form, even though one sets a single value and the other sets ten thousand. The only difference is α.

The third expression in the program is the loop that does the real work. The loop is executed k times, where k is the length of the shortest connecting path. In the example graph with 10^4 vertices and 10^6 edges, k is about 3. The looping terminates when B is labeled with a value smaller than +INF. On each iteration every vertex in G, except A, is set to one plus the minimum of its neighbors' labels. The vertex A is removed from the set being labeled, so its label remains fixed at zero.

The expression for computing the minimum of the neighbors' labels requires some explanation, because it operates on a xector of xectors. Consider first how to express the minimum of the neighbors' labels of a single vertex V:

$$(\beta\text{MIN } \alpha(\text{LABEL } \bullet(\text{NEIGHBORS } V)))$$

The `NEIGHBORS` of V are a xector of vertices, and α is used to map `LABEL` across all the elements to produce a xector of labels. This xector is then reduced by the βMIN operation to a single number. The expression in the example program works in exactly the same way, except that it is applied to a xector of vertices rather than to a single vertex. The final line of the program returns the label of B, which is the answer.

The CmLisp program corresponds closely to the informal description of Algorithm I.

2.6   Generalized Beta

The simplest use of beta is to reduce a xector to a single value. This is actually a special case of a more general operation that reduces portions of xectors and associates the results with other indices. This more general beta operation corresponds closely to the action of the message routers in the same sense that an alpha operation corresponds to the actions of the processors. It is a powerful programming tool that can be used to express some of the most basic functions of CmLisp, such as the inversion of xectors.

The general form of β takes as arguments a combining function and two xectors. It returns a third xector whose values are created from the values of the first xector and whose indexes are taken from the values of the second xector. In other words, it sends the values of the first xector to the indexes specified by the second xector. The combining function specifies how collisions are handled. In the simplest case no combining function is specified, and any collision results in an error. This corresponds to the simple two-argument β used to create a xector with a specified range and domain:

$$(\beta \text{ '[1 2 5] '[X Y Z]}) \Rightarrow \{X \rightarrow 1 \ Y \rightarrow 2 \ Z \rightarrow 5\}$$
$$(\beta \text{ '[1 2 5] '[X Z Z]}) \Rightarrow \text{error}$$

When a combining function is specified, it is used to reduce colliding values into a single value:

$$(\beta + \text{ '[1 2 5] '[X Z Z]}) \quad \Rightarrow \{X \rightarrow 1 \ Z \rightarrow 7\}$$
$$(\beta * \text{ '[1 2 5] '[X Z Z]}) \quad \Rightarrow \{X \rightarrow 1 \ Z \rightarrow 10\}$$
$$(\beta \text{PROG2 '[1 2 5] '[X Z Z]}) \Rightarrow \{X \rightarrow 1 \ Z \rightarrow 5\}$$

In this example, the function PROG2, which returns the second of two arguments, is used to make an arbitrary choice among the possible values. Because the order of reduction is unspecified, the expression can return a xector with Z mapped to either 2 or 5.

When the second xector argument is unspecified, it is taken to be a constant xector, so that all values in the xector are reduced to a single value, which is returned as the value of the expression. This special case is the single-argument beta operation that was originally introduced.

The general two-argument form of β can be used to define xector inverse as follows:

```
(DEFUN INVERSE (X)
      (β (DOMAIN X) X))
```

Because β is used without a combining function, this version of inverse produces an error if the xector is noninvertible.

The following is an example that uses both the general and single-argument forms of beta reduction to calculate the maximum number of occurrences of any single value within a xector:

```
(DEFUN ARITY (X)
      (βMAX (β+ α1 X)))
```

```
(ARITY [A B A C A B])  ⇒ 3
(ARITY {A B C D})      ⇒ 1
```

2.7 CmLisp Defines the Connection Machine

CmLisp was designed to give the programmer an expressive tool that is close to the operation of the machine yet hides most of the details of implementation. In fact, CmLisp is a good definition of what a Connection Machine really is: *A Connection Machine is the direct hardware embodiment of the*

α *and* β *operators.* Processors are α, routers are β. The contents of the memory cells are xectors.

This view of the architecture gives us a way of measuring success of an implementation: A good Connection Machine is one that implements CmLisp quickly and economically. In the following chapters I show how this can be done.

2.8   Notes

For a general introduction to Lisp, see Winston and Horn (1981). The Common Lisp dialect of Lisp on which Connection Machine Lisp is based is documented in detail in Steele and Sussman (1984), which in turn was based on MAC-LISP (Moon 1974). For an even better version of Lisp, see Steele and Sussman (1978). For a discussion of how Lisp can be compiled into machine language, see Steele (1978). For a general introduction to the terms of graph theory, see Harary (1969).

Connection Machine Lisp is a relatively conservative language for the Connection Machine. For a more radical departure from conventional languages, see Bawden (1984) and Bawden and Agre (1984). It may also be desirable to program Connection Machines in completely other types of languages; for example, functional languages (Backus 1978), constraints (Borning 1979, Sussman and Steele 1981, Sutherland 1965), actors (Hewitt 1977, Goldberg and Robson 1983, Cannon (in preparation), Weinreb and Moon 1980, Lieberman 1981), combinators (Turner 1979a, b), set operations (Schwartz 1973), communicating sequential processes (Hoare 1978), or database languages (Codd 1972, Date 1975). For another attempt to add vectorlike function calling to Lisp, see Friedman and Wise (1975).

Many of the constructs of CmLisp were in collaboration with Guy Steele, who is responsible for the first implementation.

Chapter 3

Design Considerations

In this chapter I discuss some of the issues and alternatives that arise from implementing a Connection Machine. For the most part, I ignore implementation issues that are not particular to the Connection Machine architecture. Instead I concentrate on those considerations that follow from the unusual aspects of the architecture — the fine-grain size and the general communications network.

Few parallel computers have actually been built with either fine-grain size or general communications, much less their combination. Many of the lessons learned in implementing existing machines are misleading if extrapolated to a machine of this type. In this chapter I try to outline the most important implementation issues and identify some of the trade-offs that are different for the Connection Machine. I also identify some simple measures of performance that allow a would-be Connection Machine designer to measure the success of a particular implementation. In chapter 4 I describe a specific design that is currently being built and show how it measures up under these criteria.

The issues discussed in this chapter fall roughly into three categories: the design of the processor/memory cell, the design of the communications network, and the design of the system level control. The most important issue in the design of the processor/memory cell is making a reasonable trade-off between the number and the size of the processors. This can be broken down into several questions: How many processors are needed? How big does each processor have to be? How simply can or should the individual processing element be made? For the communication network the important decision is the choice of the physical wiring pattern or topology of the routing network. There is also the question of what type of control mechanisms are to be used to route the messages. In the control area there is the question of how much autonomy should be given to the individual processing elements and how to manage the interaction between the Connection Machine and the host.

There is also a set of system issues that occur in the design of any computer but that have a different set of trade-offs for the Connection Machine. These include clocking disciplines, fault tolerance, scalability, and input/output. In section 3.12 the methods of measuring performance are discussed.

3.1   The Optimal Size of a Processor/Memory Cell

The total size and cost of Connection Machine can be controlled by varying three independent parameters: the number of processing/memory cells, the amount of memory per processor, and the size of the individual processor. From a performance standpoint, we would like all these parameters to be simultaneously as large as possible. The three goals are mutually conflicting because cost is always a limiting factor. How do we make the trade-off? Given a fixed cost and, say, a fixed processor size, we can adjust the ratio of computing power to memory size by varying the number of processors. Alternatively, we can fix the memory size and vary the number of processors by varying processor size. Which makes sense? How do we maximize the cost/performance ratio of the total machine?

The point of building a fine-grain machine in the first place is that with smaller processors it is possible to have more of them. The argument that this increases performance seems at first straightforward: If there are more processors, more operations can be performed simultaneously; thus the total time required for the computation is less. The argument, as given, does not hold up because the operations of a fine-grain processor are generally less powerful than those of its coarse-grain counterparts. For example, the fine-grain processor may use a simple, one-bit-wide arithmetic unit. Performing a 32-bit addition on such a machine requires 32 machine cycles; on a coarse-grain machine with 32-bit data paths the addition requires only a single cycle. Thus, even if it were possible to have 32 times as many fine-grain bit serial processors, there might be no speed advantage at all in the fine-grain machine. The machines would be equivalent if all the operations being performed were 32 bits wide and if the cycle times of the two machines were identical. The real speed arguments for fine-grain machines are more subtle. They hinge on the suppositions that the cost of the processor is reduced by more than the power of the instruction set and that it is possible to build fine-grain machines with faster cycle times.

The width of the processor data paths, and consequently the size of the processor is a nonlinear term in the cost/performance equation. This gives us a place to start in making a trade-off. We first decide the optimal processor size, the size with the maximum cost/performance ratio. Then we pick a memory size that matches the smallest units into which it can reasonably decompose a problem. The size of the problem then determines the number of cells. These parameters define a machine with optimal performance to solve the problem. If the cost of the machine is too great, we can decrease the number of cells and proportionally increase the amount of memory per processor. In other words, we can let one processing unit do the work of several. In this way we can make a linear trade-off between cost and performance.

In principle, this is all precise, but in practice it requires a great deal of guess work and judgment. I try to outline here some of the considerations that arise.

Serial versus Parallel Data Paths

One of the most important parameters governing the size of the processing element is the number of bits in the arithmetic unit, memory, and the connecting data paths. Here the designer can trade off one type of parallelism for another: the parallelism inherent in a wide-word operation versus the parallelism of more processors. The optimal trade-off depends partly on what applications are introduced by the machine. In symbol processing applications the narrow data paths become more favorable because operations are performed in small fields representing Boolean values, type codes, characters, and flags. A conventional wide word machine spends a relatively large percentage of its time packing and unpacking these fields into words. In addition, when operating on short fields with a parallel arithmetic unit, most of the hardware is wasted.

Even in long fixed-length arithmetic operations single-bit arithmetic logic units can be faster, assuming that it is possible to use proportionally more of them. The reason is that the speed-determining path for a parallel arithmetic unit is typically the propagation of the carry bit. In serial addition the carry bit needs to propagate over only one bit per cycle, so the cycle can be faster.

The faster-cycle argument only holds to the degree that carry propagation is the critical path. If the memory access time is the determining factor for the cycle time of the machine, then it makes sense to use a wider arithmetic unit so that its bandwidth is matched with the bandwidth of memory. Another argument in favor of wider data paths is that there is a portion of the processor logic that does not scale with the data path width. Processors with wide paths are able to spread this fixed overhead cost across a larger number of bits.

Memory Size

How much memory does a processor really need? For a Connection Machine the answer is quite different from that for other computers because data structures are not held within a single processor. Instead they are built up by tying multiple processors together. An atomic object, such as an integer, symbol, or cons cell, is held within a single processor. For the Connection Machine the question of how much memory is needed in a processor becomes: How much data is needed to store and process a single atomic data object?

Because many data structures are built from trees, each atomic object needs enough storage to store connection pointers to at least three other cells. We know from Lisp that two-pointer cons cells can be connected to form arbitrarily complex structures. Actually, each Lisp cons is connected to at least three other objects: its CAR, its CDR, and the object that points to it. Two connections are not sufficient because the only structure that could be formed would be linear chains.

The number of bits in each of these pointers depends on the address space of the machine and the mechanism for storing the type of object. But let us say for the purpose of calculations that it is 32 bits. Besides its structure pointers, a cell must also store a type code indicating what type of cell it is. Let us say that this is another 32 bits. Thus 128 bits is probably sufficient to store the internal structure of an atomic object. But we also need room to compute. Let us say that during the course of a computation an object needs to hold a temporary value for each of the three objects to which it points, plus one for itself. This doubles the amount of required storage to 256 bits. If we add another 32 bits for storing miscellaneous flags and conditions, the total comes to just under 300 bits. This is comparable to the number of bits of temporary registers that we are accustomed to in most serial machines.

Because the communications network effectively allows the use of the rest of the machine as "main memory," this is a good indication that the calculated number is correct.

According to the argument given above, a cell should require only a few hundred bits of local memory. On the other hand, the more conservative argument is "the more memory the better." This point of view has good historical support, because computer architects have almost always made the mistake of not including enough memory on their machines. But there is some ambiguity about how this lesson should be interpreted in the case of the Connection Machine. Is the important parameter the amount of memory per cell or the total memory of the machine? If it is the total memory of the machine that matters, then it may be best to solve the problem by having more cells rather than fewer larger ones.

Virtual Processors

Part of the reason for the Connection Machine architecture is that problems can be broken down into natural structural units for concurrent execution. Does the grain size of the hardware processor/memory cell need to match exactly the grain size of the natural problem unit? Fortunately, it does not. We can allow the hardware to support *virtual processors* that are larger or smaller than the physical processors of the hardware. Virtual processors larger than the hardware processors are supported by connected multiple hardware processors. Virtual processors smaller than the hardware processors are supported by dividing the memory space of each physical processor into multiple memory banks and by executing each instruction multiple times, once for each bank. This gives a linear trade-off between speed and the number of processors. The possibility of virtual cells allows the speed/size trade-off to be made by the programmer rather than by the designer of the hardware. By using multiple virtual cells per physical cell or vice versa, the programmer can choose a cell size appropriate to the application.

In the final analysis, the size of a Connection Machine is likely to be about the size and cost of a conventional computer. If the design is reasonably well balanced, about half the hardware will be devoted to memory and half to processing and communications. Connection Machines with tens to hundreds of megabytes of memory and a few million processors should be about the size and cost of a conventional mainframe computer.

Machines of about this size are more than adequate for many problems
that come up in artificial intelligence. For example, a 1000×1000 pixel
visual image has a million picture elements, so it fits naturally on a million
cell machine. Most large AI programs written in Lisp use a few hundred
thousand to a million cons cells. One would presumably use a comparable
number of processor/memory cells. The largest semantic networks, say those
used in medical diagnosis, contain a few hundred thousand links, so again the
numbers are in the right range. Of course, in the long run, as more becomes
possible, the size of the problems will grow. The beauty of this architecture
is that, unlike its serial counterparts, the Connection Machine will be able
to grow also.

3.2   The Communications Network

The most difficult technical problem in the design of a Connection Machine is
the design of the general interconnection network through which the processors communicate. The communications network represents most of the cost
of the machine, most of the power dissipation, most of the wiring, and most
of the performance limitations. This is in part because we have relatively
little experience in designing such networks, so our methods are far from
optimal. But it is also because designing such networks is fundamentally
hard; the communications network is doing most of the computation.

General communication is particularly difficult to achieve on a fine-grain
architecture because there are more processors. This limits the choice of
interconnection technologies. With only a few hundred processors to connect
it would be plausible to implement a full crossbar with a direct connection
between every pair. With a million element Connection Machine such a
crossbar would require a million squared, or 10^{12}, switch points. This is well
beyond the range of current technologies. For a Connection Machine the
number of switching elements must scale more favorably with the number of
processors.

The building blocks from which the interconnection network is constructed
are autonomous switching elements called *routers*. The routers are wired in
some relatively sparse pattern, called the *topology* of the network. In other

words, not every router is connected to every other. Processors communicate with one another through the routers, with the routers forwarding messages between processors just as the post office forwards mail from one branch to another. There are two issues in the design of such a system: One is choosing the topology for connecting the routers, and the other is choosing the algorithm for routing the messages.

3.3 Choosing a Topology

In choosing a topology, the goals can be divided roughly into two categories: cost and performance. On the performance side, we look for a combination of the following:

- Small Diameter. The diameter is the maximum number of times that a message can be forwarded between routers when traveling from one processor to another. If this distance is small, then processors are likely to be able to communicate more quickly.

- Uniformity. It is desirable that all pairs of processors communicate with equal ease or at least that the traffic patterns between all pairs of routers be reasonably balanced. This ensures that there are no bottlenecks.

- Extendability. It should be possible to build a network of any given size or, as a minimum, it should be possible to build an arbitrarily large version of the network.

- Short Wires. If the network can be efficiently embedded in two- or three-dimensional space such that all the wires are relatively short, then the physical distance between routers can be small. This means that information can propagate quickly between routers.

- Redundant Paths. If there are many possible paths between each pair of processors, a partially defective network may continue to function. Also, if a path is blocked because of traffic, a message can be directed along another route.

On the cost side we look for the following:

- Minimum Number of Wires. Each physical connection costs money. Thus if the number of wires is small, the cost is likely to be small also.

- Efficient Layout. If the topology can be tightly and neatly packed into a small space, the packaging job becomes easier.

- A Simple Routing Algorithm. Because the routers are locally controlled, this keeps down the cost of the routers.

- Fixed Degree. If each router connects to a fixed number of others, then one router design can serve for all sizes of networks.

- Fit to Available Technology. If the topology can be built easily with available components, it will be less expensive.

Notice that the wish list contains contradictions, for example, for minimum number of wires and redundant paths or for fixed degree, small diameter, and short wires. Any decision will be a compromise. Deciding which performance factors are most important is not easy. On the cost side most of the factors are difficult to measure and even more difficult to rationally trade off against one another. The fit to available technology often turns out to be one of the most important. For example, if chips come in packages with a hundred pins, a topology that requires 101 pins per chip is extremely undesirable. Printed circuit boards may cost much more if they are more than 24 inches long or may be limited to a thousand off-board connections per board. On the other hand, if someone invents a new connector or a new method of manufacturing circuit boards, the rules change. The constraints are extremely volatile. Thus the correct choice of topology and routing algorithm will change from year to year.

3.4   Tour of the Topology Zoo

The literature offers the would-be Connection Machine designer a rich choice of possible interconnection topologies, which is, of course, the last thing that the designer wants. There are grids, trees, hypercubes, omega networks, delta networks, indirect binary n-cubes, Banyan networks, hyper-toruses, twisted toruses, k-folded toruses, x-trees, shuffle exchanges, k-way shuffles, Batcher networks, Clos networks, De Brujn networks, reverse exchanges, butterfly networks, and so on. Proponents of each abound. How do we choose? Many of these networks are closely related. In fact, several networks that have been analyzed in the literature have turned out to be isomorphic. In what follows I review the major categories. Which network is optimal depends on the assumptions about requirements and available technology. References to the topologies described and machines that have used them can be in the notes at the end of this chapter.

Crossbars and Clos Networks

The simplest and most obvious network topology is to connect every node to every other node. When N is small, say, less than a hundred, this is a practical solution. In the most straightforward implementation a full crossbar requires N^2 switches, but when the connections are one-to-one, it has been shown that multistage networks with the capabilities of a crossbar can be constructed with much fewer switches. These are called *Clos* networks. For example, a five-stage Clos network with 1000 input ports requires only 146,300 switches, as opposed to the 1,000,000 required by a full crossbar.

Rings

The opposite extreme of the cost/performance trade-off is the ring topology. This is the minimal extensible topology with fixed degree. The disadvantage of these networks is that the diameter increases linearly with the number of processors, so again the topology is only practical for small N. The layout is good in two or even one dimension. The routing algorithm is extremely simple.

Trees

Another relatively inexpensive topology is the m-ary tree, where m is most commonly 2. The advantages of trees include low diameter (order log N), fixed degree, and efficient layouts in two dimensions. The primary disadvantage is the communications bottleneck at the root of the tree, but there are many algorithms with local communications patterns that do not run into this problem. Another approach is to augment the tree with additional connections to prevent congestion at the root. x-trees, for example, add connections that jump from one branch to another. Fat-trees add parallel connections to increase the capacity of links near the root.

Grids and Toruses

The two-dimensional layout of most implementation technologies naturally suggests a two-dimensional grid topology. Although the grid topology has a relatively large diameter $(2\sqrt{N})$, its topology is well matched to many problems, in particular, problems closely matched to the geometry of physical space. Examples of such problems include simulations in hydrodynamics, aerodynamics, electrodynamics, quantum chromodynamics, image processing, wire routing, and graphics. In each of these examples, calculations are often done on an n-dimensional lattice. The communications patterns are local on the lattice. Although technical constraints force a two-dimensional, or at most a three-dimensional, network, high-dimensional lattices can be efficiently projected onto such a grid. A simple and relatively common trick is to connect opposite edges, keeping the maximum wirelength short by interleaving the front and back of the torus.

Shuffle-Type Topologies

This family of networks is characterized by diameters that scale logarithmically with N. One form of this family is the butterfly communications pattern used in computing the Fast Fourier Transform. If the nodes of the butterfly network are rearranged so that each layer is drawn in the same pattern, the network is called an *omega network*. A single layer of the omega network is sometimes called a perfect shuffle or a shuffle exchange although the term is often used for the entire omega network. To make matters worse, there is also the network formed by connecting $\log N$ omega networks in series, that is, a network capable of relaying any permutation. This is also sometimes called an omega network. A somewhat more general form of the omega network was proposed independently in the telephone literature, where it is referred to as the Benes network.

A slightly repackaged form of the omega network is called the *Boolean n-cube* or *hypercube*, because of the graph formed by the corners and edges of an n-dimensional hypercube. Here $n = \log N$. The n-cube pattern can be formed by redrawing the butterfly pattern so that one corner of the cube corresponds to a row of the butterfly. A generalization of the omega or, more precisely, of the shuffle-exchange stage is the k-way shuffle, which for $k > 2$ has a smaller diameter. Other variations or isomorphisms of the omega network include the reverse exchange, and the De Brujn network.

One reason why the omega network and its relatives are so popular is that there exist simple local algorithms for routing messages through them. Omega networks are also uniform, have a reasonably small diameter, and contain redundant paths. Perhaps most importantly, they are well studied and relatively easy to visualize. One disadvantage of the n-cube version of the networks is that the degree per node grows with $\log N$. A fixed degree version of the n-cube network replaces each vertex with a ring of trivalent nodes. This version is called cube-connected cycles.

Banyan and Delta Networks

One claimed advantage of the n-cube network is the presence of redundant paths. This is also a disadvantage in the sense that redundancy adds to cost. The SW-Banyan networks are a class of logarithmic networks that contain exactly one path between any input/output pair. Delta networks are a subclass of Banyan network with particularly simple routing.

Hashnets

A final proposed answer to the question of network topology is to give up and connect everything randomly. A random network performs relatively well compared with other proposed networks, which indicates how poor our current understanding actually is. The primary advantage of hashnets, as random interconnection network have been called, is that they can be analyzed probabilistically. There is still a problem when such a network is used in multiple passes. They are also fault tolerant.

3.5 Choosing a Routing Algorithm

Along with choosing a topology for the network, we must choose an algorithm for moving information through it. This is called the *routing algorithm*.

One important decision here is whether the network is to be packet-switched or circuit-switched. The difference here is like the difference between the post office and the telephone system. The post office corresponds to packet switching, in which users of the network communicate by transmission of addressed packets. The routing and flow of the packets at any given time depends on the pattern of communication. In a circuit-switched system, such as the telephone system, two users establish a connection and are then free to communicate for as long as the connection remains established. In a circuit-switched system the routing algorithm is executed relatively rarely, when new connections are created. Once established, connections stay in place whether or not the cells are actively exchanging messages. In a packet-switched system a new route is chosen each time a message is transmitted; thus the same cells may communicate over different routes at different times. The primary advantage of circuit-switched systems is that the routing algorithm is run relatively rarely, so the routing overhead may be less. The primary advantage of a packet-switched system is that a connection consumes network resources (wires and routers) only when a message is actually being sent.

Another choice in routing algorithms is adaptive versus nonadaptive algorithms. The issue here is whether the path of a message through the network is determined solely by its source and destination (nonadaptive) or whether it can be influenced by the presence of other messages in the network (adaptive). Adaptive algorithms have, at least potentially, higher performance because they operate under fewer constraints. But they are usually more complex and more difficult to analyze.

One additional consideration in choosing a routing algorithm is ease of analysis. Again this tends to conflict with some of the other goals. Many of the networks that appear to work well in practice or simulation seem difficult to study with analytical tools. Worst-case performance, which is is usually the easiest to calculate, is often misleading because the worst case happens so seldom that it is unimportant. Random-case analysis is also unenlightening, because the patterns of communication that occur in practice are highly nonrandom. The typical case depends on the problem being solved, so it is hard to even characterize, much less analyze.

One example of the trade-off between ease of analysis and performance is the choice of adaptive versus nonadaptive algorithms. Another example is Valiant's method of probabilistically converting all patterns to the random case, at a factor of 2 cost in speed. This is accomplished by sending first to a random location and then from there to the final destination. If the communications pattern has any locality, this randomization will destroy it, so the cost may be far more than a factor of 2. Applying the randomization transformation creates a network that is easy to analyze but more than twice as slow.

3.6   Local versus Shared Control

Another implementation question in designing a Connection Machine is how much memory and control logic in each processor/memory cell should be duplicated, as opposed to being shared centrally. The two extreme answers can be characterized as multiple instruction multiple data (MIMD) and single instruction multiple data (SIMD), but there are many intermediate possibilities. The Connection Machine was originally conceived as a MIMD machine, but the first prototype was a SIMD machine. The differences are less profound than they might at first appear.

In a SIMD machine there is a single instruction stream that is broadcast to all the processor/memory cells simultaneously. Each processor has the option of executing the instruction or ignoring it, depending on its own internal state. Thus, although every processing element does not necessarily execute the same sequence of instructions, each processor is presented with the same sequence. Processors not executing must "wait out" while the active processors execute. In a MIMD machine each processor has its own independent instruction stream.

It is clear that a SIMD implementation of a Connection Machine can do anything that a MIMD implementation can and vice versa. The question is which is faster for a given amount of hardware. This depends on what level of instructions are being issued from the host computer or, to put it another way, on how much work each processor does between synchronization steps. For simple operations, say, $\alpha+$ in Connection Machine Lisp, the instruction issued by the host can correspond directly to the instruction executed by the processor. This is the SIMD case. An intermediate case is a function such as αCONS that requires some independent interpretation on the part of each processor. In the extreme MIMD case, the host issues a high-level command, such as αEVAL, that causes each processor to execute a completely different computation. Part of the trade-off between shared and local control depends on which programming style is more common.

To execute a command, such as αEVAL, from the host, each processing cell effectively needs its own program to interpret. This can be stored locally or accessed through the communications network. Different processors would have different programs. Each processing element would use a location in its local memory to point to the portion of the program being executed. In a SIMD implementation the shared instruction stream would direct each processing element to fetch the expression being evaluated and then broadcast the sequence of instructions necessary to evaluate every possible type of expression. In a MIMD implementation each processor would need only to execute the sequence of instructions relevant to its particular expression.

Even for this interpretation task, it is not clear which type of implementation has the advantage. A full MIMD machine needs to fetch fewer instructions per processor but either requires a separate program memory for each processing element or needs to move the instructions through the switching network. The former solution is extremely costly; the latter is slow. Even paying the cost of duplicated control memory does not necessarily result in a machine that is faster than its SIMD counterpart. In order to preserve memory, a MIMD machine has to place a much higher premium on the space efficiency of the code. This leads to a greater execution time. For example, the prototype Connection Machine, a SIMD implementation, uses a 96-bit-wide instruction word. A million cell MIMD machine with this wide an instruction would require more than 10^8 bits of instruction to be transferred through the interconnection network on each instruction cycle. This would be extremely inefficient if the 96-bit instruction were to specify, say, only a single bit operation. Most of the memory bandwidth, and thereby most of the power of the machine, would be used in fetching instructions. The only way a MIMD machine could be practical is with more powerful and more compact instructions. This would incur a cost in both the speed and the complexity of the processor. The argument holds even if the memory is shared and accessed through the communication network, although in this case the scarce resource is communications bandwidth rather than memory.

One potential problem with a simple-instruction wide-word SIMD implementation, is that the host may not be able to provide instructions as quickly as the processors can execute them. This problem can be alleviated by placing a special purpose *microcontroller* between the host and the Connection Machine itself. The microcontroller acts effectively as a bandwidth amplifier for the instruction stream by interpreting relatively high-level instructions from the host and converting them to sequences of the simpler instructions that are executed directly by the processors. For example, on a Connection Machine with serial ALUs, the host might specify a 32-bit addition sequence by a single command to the microcontroller, which would translate into the 32 individual bit operations to be executed directly by the cells. The microcontroller also allows critical control functions to be implemented in shared hardware rather than by repeated hardware in the individual processors or by the software in the host.

3.7 Fault Tolerance

Because a Connection Machine can potentially have an extremely large number of components, much larger than a conventional machine, even the high reliability of available microelectronic components may not be sufficient to ensure the overall reliability of the system. A machine with, say, 100 billion active components cannot reasonably be expected to operate reliably without some form of fault tolerance. There are really two issues here: soft failures and hard defects. Soft failures are dynamic errors in the system that occur during the course of a computation. An example of a commonly used method for identifying and correcting soft failures is the error correction circuitry used on dynamic memory. These methods are applicable to the Connection Machine also. Hard defects are nonfunctional components created by burnouts or manufacturing errors.

Because the Connection Machine architecture has natural units of redundancy in the processor/memory and router cells, implementations can be constructed with the capability of reconfiguring so as to continue operation even when cells fail. To implement such a system, each processor needs the ability to test its neighboring processors and associated routers. Once a defective processor or router is identified, it can be effectively isolated from the system by adjusting the behavior of all the router cells through which the defective cell communicates. A processor could be isolated, for example, by ignoring all messages that come from it. The system also needs to ensure that the isolated processor/memory cell is not built into any active data structures, so the storage allocation mechanism has to take into account the presence of defective cells. This is discussed in more detail in chapter 6. Similar techniques can be used to isolate defective routers or wires. In this case all routers that communicate with the defective component must not only ignore any messages that come from it but also ensure that any message that would normally pass through it are redirected. This assumes, of course, that the topology of the communications network includes redundant paths.

3.8   Input/Output and Secondary Storage

As in a conventional machine, it is important that a Connection Machine implementation support a balance of processing and input/output. In some applications the input/output bandwidth may actually dominate the performance of the machine, for example, in simple image processing of high resolution satellite or radar data. In other applications it may be critical to move data into and out of secondary storage, as, for example, in a database retrieval system. The success of an implementation depends on how well it fits all aspects of the application, not just the processing. The input/output performance can become extremely important, particularly if this portion of the machine is poorly designed.

Fortunately, the Connection Machine architecture provides two natural possibilities for high-bandwidth input/output ports: through the communications network and directly to the individual processors. The former solution is more flexible, the latter simpler. Even with a one-bit channel per processor, a reasonable size Connection Machine can transfer data at a rate much higher than can be supported by conventional peripherals, so the difficult problem is in the design of the peripherals. This goes beyond the scope of this discussion.

3.9   Synchronous versus Asynchronous Design

In most modern machine designs the operation of all components is synchronized to a single central clock. The primary reason for this is simplicity of design. One problem with synchronous clocking is that, as machines grow physically larger, it becomes increasingly difficult to synchronize the components in different parts of the machine. The signal propagation skews between one part of the machine and another become significant. Also, there is some time penalty for synchronization because all components must operate at the speed of the slowest. An additional argument against synchronous design is that it is fundamentally impossible to incorporate asynchronous real world input without introducing the possibility of synchronizer failures.

How does the Connection Machine architecture affect the issue of synchronous versus asynchronous design? On one hand, it raises the possibilities of running into some of the limitations of synchronous design by allowing the possibility of constructing arbitrarily large machines. On the other hand, it alleviates some of these problems through the uniformity of its architecture. Although a Connection Machine can be large, the local neighborhoods over which synchronization must be maintained are limited by the topology of the communications network; synchronization needs to be maintained only locally, between directly communicating components, rather than globally. Also, because all components are essentially identical, operating at the speed of the slowest is no great penalty. These factors seem to favor synchronous design.

3.10   Numeric versus Symbolic Processing

What is the difference between a "number cruncher" and a computer designed for processing symbols? There is a real distinction here, because many architectures operate extremely well for one type of operation and poorly for others, and a few perform reasonably well at both. All data operated on by a computer is internally represented by numbers, so it is not exactly a distinction between numbers and symbols but between different types of numbers and different mixes of operations on them. Number crunchers are optimized primarily for arithmetic operations on large, usually floating-point numbers. In a typical symbolic application, multiplication and division are rare, and floating-point numbers are even rarer. Symbolic processors are optimized instead for memory reference, flow control, and secondarily for logical/arithmetic operations on small variable-length fixed-point numbers. In a typical symbolic application a large percentage of the machine's time is spent in the overhead of subroutine calls, set up for nonlocal exits, context switching, and other operations of control.

There is also a difference between symbolic and numeric computation in the complexity of data structures. In symbolic applications data structures tend to be complex, linked pointer patterns, scattered through memory. In numeric applications the most common data structure is a linearly allocated array or vector. This regularity allows for the efficient use of vector operations.

In a Connection Machine these issues affect the optimal implementation of both the processor/memory cell and the communications network. If the intended applications for the machine involve intensive use of floating-point numbers, then the individual processing element may require special floating-point hardware. If it is intended for symbolic applications, then the ability to manipulate small variable length fields becomes important. These trade-offs are similar to those made in the conventional computer, except that in the Connection Machine the cost of any hardware added per processor must be multiplied by the number of processors; thus the addition of each feature is more expensive. In the communications section of the machine, the numeric/symbolic distinction is significant primarily because of the relative regularity of communications patterns that are likely to occur. The numeric patterns tend to be more structured, and the symbolic patterns tend to be more random. Some interconnection network designs perform well on one type of pattern but not on the other.

3.11   Scalability and Extendability

One advantage of the Connection Machine architecture is that potentially it allows significant increases in the size of the machine without significant redesign of the components. The architecture is *scalable*. It should be possible to build Connection Machines that are ten or even hundreds of times larger than existing machines at a comparable increase in cost. It is even possible to build a Connection Machine that is incrementally scalable, that is, *extendable*. Such a machine can be expanded by adding additional processor/memory communications units into an existing machine in much the same way that additional memory units can be added to a conventional computer. If the system is designed correctly, the machine could be extended in this way without even a change in software.

Scalable and extendable machines have a potential cost advantage because they are made of large numbers of replicated parts that can be mass produced efficiently and because the design cost can be amortized over larger numbers of configuration. The disadvantage of a scalable machine is that the extra "hooks" left for expansion, such as extra bits in the address space or extra connectors on the backplane, add to the cost and complexity of design.

3.12   Evaluating Success

Given this wide range of options for implementing a Connection Machine, how can we effectively compare and evaluate various alternate designs? Part of the answer is hard and depends on how well the implementation matches what problems. This question probably has no simple answer, except where one implementation can efficiently simulate another. But there is another part of the answer that is easier to measure. Does the implementation have sufficient raw computing power? Such power will not be of much use if it cannot be efficiently applied to a problem, but it is worth checking to see if the power is there to be applied at all. This section suggests some simple measures of raw computing power. It does not attempt to answer the application-specific questions or the more general question of range of applicability.

Measure I: Size of Memory

Memory size should be the least controversial of the measures. A machine cannot solve a problem if it cannot hold it. Memory is measured in bits, so a machine with 8K of 64-bit words is equivalent under this measure to a machine with 64K of 8-bit words. The one thing that may cause evaluation problems is how to count various forms of secondary storage. Do we count the secondary storage on a machine with virtual cells? This decision can be made either way, but a consistent definition of memory should be used for all performance measures for a given machine. For most implementations it is appropriate to count only the amount of random access memory.

Measure II: Memory Bandwidth

Having defined memory, the definition of memory bandwidth is straightforward. How many bits can be moved to and from the memory per second? A bit counts as being moved from the memory if it is stored in another memory or fed to a processing cell. Similarly, a bit only counts as moving to the memory if a new value is written over an old one. This prevents, for example, the inclusion of refresh cycles into the memory bandwidth calculation.

Measure III: Processing Bandwidth

How many bits go into and out of arithmetic-logic units per second? Here there is no distinction as to whether the operations being performed are simple Booleans or floating-point multiplications. We are not trying to measure the quality of the instruction set. Again the count is of bits, not words, so a serial machine with a 10-nsec ALU cycle time counts the same as a 100-bit machine with a 1-μsec cycle. Also all the bits going into and out of the arithmetic-logic unit are counted, so a machine that can operate with four ALU inputs and two outputs counts as twice the measure of a similar machine with two inputs and one output. This measure differs from memory bandwidth only if there is some kind of local caching or register.

Measure IV: Communication Bandwidth

In many applications the performance of the machine is limited by the communications requirements among the individual processing elements. The communications bandwidth is intended to be a measure of this capacity. The communications bandwidth is defined as the total memory size of the machine divided by the time required to perform an arbitrary permutation on all bits in the memory. For most machines this number depends considerably on the permutation, so it makes sense to look at both the average and the worst case. In particular applications it also makes sense to ask about particular classes of permutations, such as a two-dimensional grid permutation or a perfect shuffle permutation of 32-bit words.

Measure V: Input and Output Bandwidths

Input and output bandwidths are calculated in a manner analogous to memory bandwidth. Bandwidth to secondary storage is included.

These measures provide a simple mechanism for comparing Connection Machine implementations. They may even provide a way of comparing computers in general, especially parallel computers. Notice that all the measures make sense even for a single processor machine. A communications bandwidth, as defined, is proportional to a memory bandwidth for a conventional processor. For idealized parallel machines with shared memory, such as Schwartz's paracomputer (Schwartz 1980b), all the numbers scale linearly with the number of processors. This fits well with our intuitive measure of computing power. Unfortunately, these measures do not address the more interesting and difficult questions of how well the power can be applied to a given application or over what range of applications the architecture is efficient. Simple answers to these questions are hard to find.

3.13   Notes

For a general review of circuit connection topologies, see Broomell and Heath (1983), Thompson (1978), or Benes (1965) (from the standpoint of telephone switching systems). For analysis of logarithmic-type networks, see Lang and Stone (1976) (shuffle-exchange), Lawrie (1975) (omega networks), Pease (1968) (perfect shuffle), Pease (1968) (indirect n-cube), Wittie (1981) and Valiant (1982a) (n-cubes), Kruskal and Snir (1982) (Banyan networks), Schwartz (1980b) (perfect shuffle), and Benes (1965) (Benes networks and Clos networks). For a demonstration of the equivalence of many of these, see Parker (1980) and Snir (1982).

For networks based on tree structures, see Browning (1980), Goodman and Despain (1980) (hypertrees), and Sequin and coworkers (1978 and 1982) (augmented trees). Also, Leiserson (1985) introduced a structure called a *fat tree* that can efficiently simulate any other physically realizable topology. For a discussion of communication in gridlike machines, see Orcutt (1976). Another intriguing possibility for switching topologies that are optimal in a certain sense are Moore graphs (Hoffman and Singleton 1960). For a discussion of the topologies in the human brain, see Sholl (1956).

Wu and Liu (1981) give an analytic comparison of trees and n-cubes. For analysis of various topologies in the context of a specific database problem, see Goodman and Despain (1980). Garner and Squire (1963) compare n-cubes and two-dimensional grids.

For introductions to queueing theory, see Gross and Harris (1974) and Kleinrock (1973, 1976). For specific analyses, see Kleinrock (1964) and Ziegler (1971) (grids). For actual measurements of queueing delays, see Cole (1971). For a specific application or another specific example of queueing, see Gerla (1973).

For a discussion of the merits of synchronous versus asynchronous design and the local synchronization, see Seitz (1980). The relative merits of SIMD versus MIMD versus multiple SIMD machines are discussed in Siegel et al. (1981).

Chapter 4

The Prototype

In this chapter I describe a specific Connection Machine implementation, a 64K prototype machine currently being constructed at Thinking Machines Corporation, Cambridge, Massachusetts. The prototype is called the CM-1. Its primary purposes are to evaluate the Connection Machine architecture and to provide a tool for the development of software. Speed of operation was not a primary design goal; instead, the emphasis was on flexibility. We were interested in evaluating the architecture, not the quirks of a particular implementation. Many of the functions were implemented in a general elegant form, even at a cost in speed.

The CM-1 contains 64K (2^{16}) cells, each with 4K (2^{12}) bits of memory and a simple serial arithmetic logic unit. The processors are connected by a packet-switched network based on a Boolean n-cube topology and use an adaptive routing algorithm. All processors execute instructions from a single stream generated by a microcontroller under the direction of a conventional host. The machine, including the microcontroller, processor/memory cells, and communication network is packaged in a cube roughly 1.3 m on a side.

In conventional terms the machine has a peak instruction rate (32-bit additions) of about 1000 MIPS (millions of instructions per second). In terms of the evaluation criteria set forth at the end of the last chapter, the machine measures as follows:

- Size of Memory: 2.5×10^8 bits

- Memory Bandwidth: 2.0×10^{11} bits/second

- Processor Bandwidth: 3.3×10^{11} bits/second

- Communications Bandwidth:

    - Worst Case: $\approx 3.2 \times 10^7$ bits/second

    - Typical Case: $\approx 1.0 \times 10^9$ bits/second

  – 2-D Pattern: $\approx 3.3 \times 10^{10}$ bits/second

  – FFT Pattern: $\approx 5.0 \times 10^{10}$ bits/second

• Input/Output Bandwidth: 5.0×10^8 bits/second

In this chapter, I will describe in detail the design of the processor/memory cell and the design of the interconnection network. I also describe the operation of the microcontroller and give an overview of the packaging of the system.

4.1   The Chip

The key component from which CM-1 is constructed is a custom designed VLSI chip that contains 16 processor cells and one router unit of the packet switch communications network. It contains three principal sections: the control unit, the processor array, and the router. The control unit decodes *nanoinstructions* coming in over the *instruction pins* and produces signals that control the operation of the processor and the router. All actions of the control unit are synchronized to an externally supplied *clock*. There are 16 individual serial processing units on the chip. Under the direction of the control unit these processing elements take data from external memory, perform arithmetic and logical operations on the data, and store the results in memory. All transfers to and from memory take place over the bidirectional *memory pins*. Each processor has its own set of internal flags for storing intermediate bits of state during a computation.

The router is responsible for routing messages between chips and delivering them to the destination specified by the address. The router communicates with the routers of other chips through the bidirectional *cube pins*. The router has three sections: the *injector*, which transmits new messages into the network; the *heart*, which forwards messages between chips; and the *ejector*, which receives and delivers messages to the appropriate processing element. The router is also directly connected to the off-chip memory through the memory pins, which it uses for buffering messages. All operations of the router are controlled by the control unit.

There is also a second gridlike communications system provided on the chip for local or highly structured communications patterns. This communication system does not involve the router. Instead each processor communicates directly with its North, East, West and South neighbors. On chip, the processors are connected in a 4 × 4 grid. This two-dimensional grid pattern can be extended across multiple chips by connecting the *NEWS pins* of adjacent chips.

The chip provides two different mechanisms for returning information to the microcontroller. First, the external memory can be read back over the instruction pins. Second, any of the 16 processing elements can assert a signal to be sent back over the *global pin* or the *error pin*. The signal sent off the chip is the logical OR of the assertions of the individual processors. In addition to the main blocks described above, the chip also contains circuitry for checking various parities, correcting errors in memory, and diagnosing faults within the chip.

The processor/router chip is implemented on CMOS die about 1 cm^2 in area. There are approximately 50,000 active devices. The chip dissipates approximately 1 W of power running at a clock rate of 4 MHz. It is packaged in a 68-pin square ceramic carrier.

Each Connection Machine chip has associated with it 4K × 4 static memory chips. This unit of one Connection Machine chip and four memory chips accounts for more than 90 percent of the circuitry of the Connection Machine. Thirty-two of these units are packaged onto a single printed circuit board, called a *module*. Each module contains 512 processor/memory cells. The modules are plugged into *backplanes* of 16 modules each, and two of these backplanes are mounted into a single rack. Four racks are placed together into roughly the shape of a cube to form the 64K-processor machine.

The hierarchy of the packaging follows closely the topology of the Boolean n-cube. The first five dimensions of the cube are connected within a module, the next four within a backplane, and the final three within the racks. Each of the 12 edges of this top level cube consists of 8,192 signal ground pairs. These signals are run on controlled impedance flat cables. The remaining dimensions are connected on the printed circuitry of the modules and backplanes. The machine is air cooled and dissipates about 12,000 W when operating on a 4 MHz clock.

4.2   The Processor Cell

The individual processing cell of the CM-1 is extremely simple. It has only 8 bits of internal state information (flags). All its data paths are only one bit wide. A block diagram of the processing element is shown in figure 4.1.

The basic operation of the processing element is to read two bits from the external memory and one flag, combine them according to a specified logical operation producing two bits of results, and to write the resulting bits into the external memory and an internal flag, respectively. This sequence of operations requires three clock cycles, one for each reference to the external memory. During these three clock cycles, the microcontroller specifies the following parameters of the operation:

- **A-address** (12 bits) specifies the external memory address from which the first bit is read. This is also the address to which the memory output of the Arithmetic/Logic Unit is written.

- **B-address** (12 bits) specifies the external memory address from which the second bit is read.

- **Read-Flag** (4 bits) specifies one of the 16 (8 general purpose, 8 special purpose) flags from which the F input of the Arithmetic/Logic Unit is to be taken.

- **Write-Flag** (4 bits) specifies one of the 16 flags to which the flag output of the Arithmetic/Logic Unit is written.

- **Condition-Flag** (4 bits) specifies which of the flags is to be used to conditionalize the operation (see Conditionalization, the next subsection).

- **Condition Sense** (1 bit) selects either the 1 or the 0 condition for instruction execution.

- **Memory Truth Table** (8 bits) specifies which of the 256 possible Boolean functions is to be used to compute the memory output from the three inputs to the Arithmetic/Logic Unit.

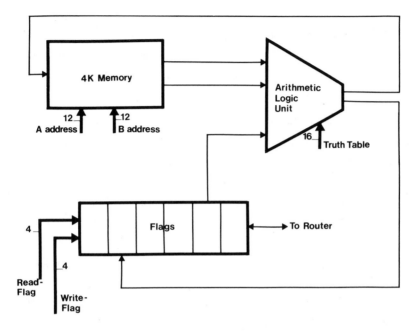

Figure 4.1   Block diagram of a single Connection Machine processing element.

- **Flag Truth Table** (8 bits) specifies which of the 256 possible Boolean functions is to be used to compute the flag output from the three inputs to the Arithmetic/Logic Unit.

- **NEWS Direction** (2 bits) specifies whether data is to move across the two-dimensional grid in a North, East, West, or South direction during this instruction. (This path is used for input/output.)

These parameters can be specified in any combination. This results in an extremely simple but overly general instruction set. For example, it is possible to specify any of the 65,536 (2^{32}) possible Arithmetic/Logic Unit functions for three inputs or two outputs by giving the truth tables for the memory and flag outputs. This allows not only the specification of the standard arithmetical and logical functions, such as add, subtract, and or and xor, but also thousands of relatively useless variants. This is an example of the kind of generality provided by the prototype. Rather than try to guess which operations will be most useful, we have included them all. Obviously this type of generality incurs a cost, in this case in the speed of the Arithmetic/Logic Unit and in the width of the microcode (pins and wires). On future machines it will probably be desirable to optimize with a more restricted instruction set. Notice that with the current scheme, however, that the Connection Machine processor cell is the ultimate reduced instruction set (RISC) computer with only one extremely powerful instruction.

Conditionalization

All processors receive the same instruction from the control unit, but a processor has the option of executing an instruction or not, depending on the internal state of one of the processor flags. The CONDITION-FLAG parameter specifies which flag is to be used for this purpose, and the CONDITION-SENSE parameter specifies how this flag is to be interpreted. If the condition sense parameter is a 0, then the flag must be a 0 in order for the instruction to be executed. If the condition sense is 1, then the flag must be 1 also. Conditionalization is done on a per processor basis, so that some processors can write a new value, whereas others may not.

The Flags

There are sixteen flags associated with each processor. Eight of these flags are general purpose one-bit registers. They have no predefined function imposed by the hardware and are typically used for storing things such as the carry bit between successive cycles of a serial addition operation. The other eight flags in the processing element have special purposes assigned by the hardware. Some can be read and written, such as the general purpose flags. Others can only be read. These flags provide the interface between the processing element and the router and between processing elements through the North, East, West, South (NEWS) connections.

The following flags have special functions:

- **NEWS Flag**. This flag contains information written from the FLAG OUTPUT of the Arithmetic/Logic Unit of the North, East, West, or South neighbor. Which one depends on the NEWS-DIRECTION parameter to the instruction.

- **Cube Flag**. This flag reads directly off one of the cube pins connecting to other chips. This allows the programmer to bypass the router and to access n-cube neighbors directly in much the same way as the NEWS flag accesses the two-dimensional neighbors. This is used primarily for diagnosis.

- **Router-Data Flag**. This flag is used for sending data to and receiving data from the router. The format of the message passing through this flag is essentially the address followed by the data (see figure 4.2).

- **Router-Acknowledge Flag**. This read-only flag is a handshaking bit sent back from the router to acknowledge the successful transmission of a message.

- **Daisy-Chain Flag**. This read-only flag reads the flag output of the processor ahead on the on-chip daisy chain. It effectively allows the 16 on-bit processor/memory on a chip to be connected to a single 16-bit processor/memory cell.

- **Long-Parity Flag**. This writable flag automatically keeps track of the parity of the data in a processor's external memory. It is used in conjunction with the *short parity bit* stored in external memory to allow single bit error correction within the memory.

- **Input Flag**. The input flag reads the reserved input pin of the chip.

- **Zero Flag**. This read-only flag will always read 0. By convention, operations that do not write a flag specify the zero flag in the write flag parameter.

These special purpose flags and the eight general purpose flags are accessible to the programmer through the microcode but are not visible from the macrocode.

4.3   The Topology

Each router handles messages for 16 processing cells. The communications network of the CM-1 is formed by 4,096 routers connected by 24,576 bidirectional wires. The routers are wired in the pattern of a Boolean n-cube.

The address of the routers within the network depend on their relative position within the n-cube. Assume that the 4,096 routers have addresses 0 through 4,095. Then the router with address i will be connected to the router with address j if and only if $|i - j| = 2^k$ for some integer k. In this case, we say that the routers are connected along the kth dimension. Geometrically, the Boolean n-cube can be interpreted as a generalization of a cube to an n-dimensional Euclidean space. Each dimension of the space corresponds to one bit position in the address. An edge of the cube pointing along the kth dimension connects two vertices whose addresses differ by 2^k, that is, they differ in the kth bit of the address. Because any two 12-bit addresses differ by no more than 12 bits, any vertex of the cube can be reached from any other by traveling over no more than 12 edges. Each router is no more than 12 wires away from a neighboring router. Smaller networks can be constructed by deleting nodes from the 12-cube. Networks with more than 2^{12} nodes would require a larger router, although this would be a simple extension of the current design.

The operations of the router can be divided into five categories: *injection, delivery, forwarding, buffering,* and *referral*. The 16 processors that a router serves can send new messages into the network by the process of injection.

P	data (m bits)	1	address (12 bits)

Figure 4.2 Message format.

Messages can also come in from other routers. Some of these messages are destined for other procesors served by the router. The process by which a router removes a message from the network and sends it to the processor for which it is destined is called delivery. If an injected message is going somewhere outside the cluster of 16, it must be forwarded. Incoming messages can also need forwarding. If several messages want to be forwarded over the same wire, they can need to be buffered by the router. Buffering can also be necessary if several messages need to be delivered at once. If the buffer is full, then the router may need to refer a message to another router. This process is similar to forwarding except that it may not bring a message closer to its final destination.

The algorithm used by the router can be broken into repeating cycles called *petit cycles*. Each petit cycle can be divided further into 12 *dimension cycles*, one for each dimension of the router. During a petit cycle, messages are moved across each of the 12 dimensions in sequence. Each of these motions along a single dimension is called a dimension cycle. In a Boolean n-cube a message can be no more than one step away from its destination per dimension; thus all messages are delivered within a single petit cycle unless they are delayed by traffic. Messages that are delayed by traffic are delayed by at least one full petit cycle because there is only one chance to move along each dimension during a petit cycle.

The injection process involves a simple handshake between processor and router. A processor initiates a message by sending a valid message packet to its router data flag in the format shown in figure 4.2, consisting of an address, followed by a 1 for formatting, followed by the data, followed by a parity bit. The data portion of the message can be of any length so long as the lengths of all the messages in the network are the same. The router can accept or reject a message based on its current loading. This information is then transmitted back to the processor through the router acknowledge flag. If a message is rejected, then the processor attempts to retransmit it at a later time.

Message injection can be initiated by a processor at the beginning of each petit cycle. The number of messages accepted by a router during a petit cycle depends on the number of buffers that it had free at the begining of the petit cycle. A router will accept no more messages than it has free buffers, and in no case will it accept more than four messages in a single petit cycle.

The address of a message can be divided into three portions: the address of the processor within a router cluster, the address of the router, and the address of the memory within the processor.

Except for delivery, the router is concerned only with the router portion of the address. This portion is specified relative to the address of router in which the message currently resides. For example, when the address is 0, then the message is to be delivered to one of the directly connected processors. If the address is 000001000100, then the message must move across two wires to reach its destination. Each time a message is moved from one router to another, the address is updated to maintain its relative address with respect to its destination. Because each bit of the address corresponds to one dimension of the n-cube, each time a message moves along a dimension, one bit of the address must change. When the address becomes 0, the message has arrived.

During the first dimension cycle, the router can choose a single message to be sent across the wire corresponding to dimension 0. In general, during the kth dimension cycle, each node chooses a message to be sent across the kth wire. A node makes this choice by looking at the kth bit of each message. Any message with a 1 in the kth bit needs to move along the kth dimension. The router searches all messages it has, including newly injected messages, messages buffered from a previous petit cycle, and messages that arrived during earlier dimension cycles of the current petit cycle. The router searches them in order so that if there are several messages with the kth address bit set, the one that has been at the node the longest will have the highest priority. The chosen message, if there is one, will be sent along the wire kth direction, with the kth address bit complemented to preserve address relativity.

During a petit cycle, this process of choosing a message is repeated 12 times, once for each dimension. All messages are taken to their final destinations unless they are delayed by traffic. For example, if there were only one message, it would never be delayed and would always reach its destination in a single petit cycle. When there are many messages in the network, several messages often need to travel over the same wire. All but one will be delayed, so it can take some messages several petit cycles to reach their destinations. If a message is blocked along some dimension, it can make progress along other dimensions during the same cycle, but because a message can only move along the kth dimension during the kth dimension cycle, a blocked message must be delayed by at least a full message cycle. (Remember that the dimensions are completely orthogonal, so that no amount of motion in other dimensions can compensate for a missing step along a particular direction. A blocked message has to wait for the next opportunity to move in the blocked dimension, which comes a full petit cycle later.)

Each message is checked for a zero router address at the end of a petit cycle. Messages with zero addresses have arrived and are delivered to the processor. If a node has messages with nonzero addresses or if it has too many zero-addressed messages to deliver at once, these messages are held in a buffer until the next petit cycle. Messages delayed by higher priority messages during the preceding petit cycle will have nonzero addresses.

As I have described the algorithm so far, a message can move only toward its destination. Because at least one message at each node is guaranteed to make progress during each cycle (the message of highest priority), the network as a whole always makes progress. It is easy to see that, if we stop injecting new messages into the network, all pending messages will be delivered within a number of cycles proportional to the number of pending messages. Assume that there are k messages in the network. The maximum distance between routers in the network is 12; thus the total distance of all messages from their respective destinations cannot be greater than $12k$. Because messages never move away from their destinations and because at least one message per occupied router must make progress during each cycle, the total distance must decrease by at least one message per cycle. Within $12k$ cycles it must reach zero, in which case all messages must be at their destinations.

A problem with the algorithm as described so far is that there is no obvious bound on the number of messages that may need to be buffered at a node between petit cycles. The router is hardware limited to a fixed buffer capacity. The number of buffers (seven in the CM-1) is large enough so that the router almost never runs short of storage, but an additional mechanism has been provided for dealing with the overflow case should it occur. This mechanism is called *referral.* When a router's buffers become full, excess messages are referred over unused wires to adjoining routers. Because there are as many outgoing as incoming wires, it is always possible to find an unused wire on which to refer a message.

The referral process works like this. During a petit cycle a node may receive up to 12 incoming messages, one during each dimension cycle. The algorithm assumes that this worst case will happen. Let k be the number of empty buffers at the beginning of the petit cycle. So long as at least $12 - k$ messages are sent away from the router, it will be able to buffer the remainder. The router can receive messages during the first k dimension cycles without danger of overflow because it always has the option of forcing out a message during each of the $12 - k$ remaining cycles. Let j be the number of messages the router sends out during these k cycles. These transmissions allow the router to wait an additional j dimension cycles before forcing messages. More messages can be transmitted during these j cycles, postponing the problem even further.

In general, the router is safe on the ith cycle if the number of free buffers plus the number of messages it has sent out is greater then $12 - i$. Whenever this condition fails, the router must send a message on every wire in every dimension cycle for the remainder of the petit cycle. This is accomplished by forcing out the lowest priority message, i.e., the message that arrived most recently, whenever none of the other messages needs to move over the current dimension. In other words, the lowest priority message can be referred to another router. The referred message still contains the address of its intended destination, so it will be delivered.

The referred message has an address bit complemented from a 0 to a 1. In other words, the message moves one step farther from its destination. Simulations indicate that this occasional backstep is not a significant performance problem. However, it does invalidate the argument for a linear time bound given previously, which depends on the monotonic property of the routing algorithm. I leave this as an unsolved problem.

The same mechanisms that route a message around a busy wire can be used to delete defective nodes and wires from the system. All wires leading to a deleted node are simply declared to be permanently busy by its neighbors. Any transmissions coming from the deleted node are ignored. We must also assume that there are no messages destined for the deleted node. Under this assumption, any message that wishes to travel over one of the falsely busy wires also has other directions in which it wishes to travel, so it will not get stuck. The referral mechanism continues to work because, although we have removed a possible direction of referral, we have also removed a source of messages. Defective wires can also be effectively deleted by deleting a node at one end of the wire.

When a message finally reaches its destination router, it is delivered to the appropriate processor by writing into the processor's memory. The number of messages that a router can deliver during a single petit cycle depends on how multiple messages traveling to the same memory are to be combined. If no two messages are destined to the same address or if it is acceptable to combine the data of colliding messages by an inclusive-or operation, then up to seven messages can be delivered simultaneously. If some other combining function is desired, for example, adding the data fields, then the router will only deliver one message at a time. Both modes of operation are supported.

4.4   Routing Performance

The performance of the routing algorithm is dependent on the number and the pattern of messages. The traffic on the wires between the routers tends to be the limiting factor, although for extremely local message patterns, the communications bandwidth can be limited by the maximum rate of injection; and near the end of a delivery cycle the maximum rate of delivery becomes important. I discuss these three cases separately.

Bandwidth-Limited Message Patterns

In the case of random or nonlocal message patterns, the average delivery rate is slightly less than two messages per node per petit cycle. It can be shown by counting the number of wires used that the average delivery rate cannot be greater than this value. The distance that a message must travel in the network is equal to the number of 1 bits in the relative address. A random message contains $n/2$ 1's in the addresses, where n is the number of address bits and $N = 2^n$ is the number of routers.

A maximum of one message can travel over a wire during each petit cycle, and only one bit in the address of a message can change per wire over which it travels. Because there are $nN = n2^n$ wires, the maximum rate at which the network can change 1's into 0's is $n2^n$ bits per petit cycle. Because the network has limited storage, the number of 1's cannot grow arbitrarily large; thus after some startup time the maximum injection rate of 1's cannot be greater than $n2^n$ per cycle, or n per node per cycle. Because a random message has an average of $n/2$ 1 bits, there must not be more than two injected per cycle.

We can use this number to calculate the maximum sustained bandwidth of the network for random messages. A petit cycle for a k-bit message requires k machine cycles, plus some overhead. By making the messages long, we can make the overhead insignificant. (Even for the smallest messages it is less than 50 percent.) A machine cycle takes about 5×10^{-7} sec. Because a maximum of $2 \times N = 2^{n+1}$ k-bit messages are passing into the network each petit cycle, the maximum steady-state network bandwidth is

$$\frac{\text{bits}}{\text{seconds}} = \frac{k \times 2^{n+1}}{k \times 5 \times 10^{-7}} = \frac{2^{n+1}}{5 \times 10^{-7}}$$

This upper bound does not take into account two potential inefficiencies. First, it may be impossible to use every wire in every cycle. Second, if the buffers fill, a message will actually have to take a step away from its destination. We can make this arbitrarily unlikely by deliberately running the network lightly loaded. Including a loading factor in the calculation also takes into account the unused wires. Experiments show that a realistic loading factor is 50 percent. That is, about half of the wires are unused on each cycle. Thus the true bandwidth is more like $10^6 \times 2^{n-1}$:

$$0.5 \times \left\{ \frac{2^{n+1}}{5 \times 10^7} \right\} = 10^6 \times 2^{n+1} \text{ bits/sec.}$$

Thus for the 4K-router prototype, the sustained random-message bandwidth is about 10^{10} bits/sec. This number fits well with the results of the simulation.

Local Message Patterns

If the messages tend to be local, that is, if the average number of 1's per address is less than $n/2$, the bandwidth can be increased. If it increases sufficiently, the maximum rate of message injection per node can become a limiting factor. In the prototype the maximum injection rate is limited to no more than four messages per node per cycle. Because wire loading is not the limitation, we do not need to add an inefficiency factor as in the random case, so we might expect the sustained bandwidth to be about four times higher for local message patterns. Again, this agrees well with the simulation.

Because the local message pattern has a higher bandwidth, it can be desirable, when possible, to allocate storage in such a way as to localize communication. Several of the storage allocation schemes discussed in chapter 6 tend to do this. It is not, however, always possible. The local neighborhood of a node is small compared with the size of the network. Almost all the potential storage is an average distance away. The number of nodes at distance d is $\binom{n}{d}$, so most of the nodes are at $d = n/2$.

Local message patterns do occur quite frequently in particular algorithms. For example, in beta reduction each message has only a single 1 in the address. This type of communications pattern is particularly simple and is limited strictly by the injection rate to four messages per cycle. Many other patterns, including two- and three-dimensional grids, butterflies, and trees, have local embedding on an n-cube.

The Tail Message Pattern

The limitations on bandwidth given by the wire and injection limits apply when the router is in a steady state. A typical message cycle involves sending a burst of messages. There are two times when the interconnection network is not at all steady: at the beginning and at the end of the burst. (See figure 4.3.) During every start of a cycle, when the messages are entering an empty network, the statistics of wire use and blockage are favorable compared with the steady state. Because this period does not last long, it does not significantly affect the total time of the burst. The more important effect is at the tail. Here the network is essentially delivery rate limited. The entire network waits while the last few stragglers find their way home. The length of this tail depends on the total number of messages delivered to a node during a burst. Fortunately, in regard to this statistic, even the random message pattern of the Connection Machine is not truly random. This is because each router node serves a fixed number of processing elements and because each processing element receives only one (or sometimes two) messages per burst. Thus the random message pattern is restricted to a pattern of messages, called an *h*-permutation (Valiant 1982b), in which no node can receive more than *h* messages per burst. By using this fact, we can easily put an upper limit on the number of petit cycles in the tail:

$$T_{tail} \leq mh/d$$

where *m* is the number of processors per node (16), *h* is the maximum number of messages destined to each processor (typically one), and *d* is the maximum number of deliveries per node per cycle (seven). We are assuming here that the wires are not a limit, which is a realistic approximation during the lightly loaded tail period.

If we assume that the number of messages scale with the size of the network, then for a sufficiently large network bad cases are almost guaranteed. If there are *n* processors per chip, each of which can receive a message with independent probability *P*, then the probability $P(tail \geq k)$ that one chip out of *N* receives at least *k* messages is

$$P(tail \geq k) = 1 - \left(\sum_{x=0}^{k-1} \binom{n}{x} p^x (1-p)^{n-x} \right)^N \approx 1 - e\left(-N \sum_{x=k}^{n} \binom{n}{x} p^x (1-p)^{n-x}\right).$$

Thus a bad case almost always occurs if

$$\sum_{x=n}^{n} \binom{n}{x} p^x (1-p)^{n-x} > 1/N.$$

For the prototype, $n = 16$ and $N = 4096$.

It is therefore relatively easy to estimate the delivery time for a large random permutation of *M* messages by adding the steady state or injection time and the tail time.

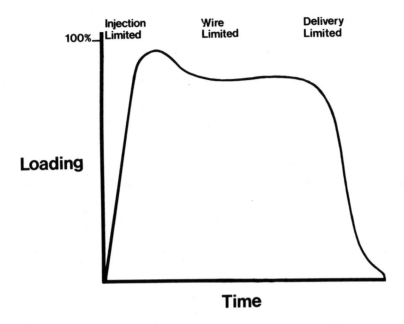

Figure 4.3 A typical pattern of loading in the network over time during one delivery cycle.

Table 4.1 Relationships among the Four Types of Instruction Sets.

Section	Executes	Produces
Host	Host Code	Macro Code
Microcontroller	Micro Code	Nano Code
CM Cell	Nano Code	Bits

4.5   The Microcontroller

The host talks to the processor/memory cells through a microcontroller. The purpose of the microcontroller is to act as a bandwidth amplifier between the host and the processors. Because the processors execute an extremely simple bit-at-a-time instruction set, they are able to execute instructions at a higher rate than the host is able to specify. Instead, the host specifies higher-level *macroinstructions*, which are interpreted by the microcontroller to produce *nanoinstructions*. It is the nanoinstructions that are executed directly by the processors. The instructions executed by the microcontroller that specify how this interpretation is to take place are called *microinstructions*.

Thus there are four instruction sets to be kept straight: host-instructions (executed by the host), macroinstructions (interpreted by the microcontroller), microinstructions (executed by the microcontroller), and nanoinstructions (executed by the individual processor memory cells). The relationships for these four instruction sets are summarized in table 4.1. Only the nanoinstruction set is described in this document.

Between the host and the microcontroller is a pair of first-in/first-out buffers (FIFOs) that buffer macroinstructions going to the microcontroller and data returning to the host. These buffers allow the Connection Machine to operate asynchronously with the host. They also allow the host and Connection Machine to maintain a higher average instruction bandwidth when executing a mixture of simple and complex macroinstructions. This is because simple macroinstructions can be executed by the Connection Machine more quickly than they can be generated by the host, whereas the reverse is true for complex macroinstructions. The FIFOs allow the Connection Machine to keep busy so long as the average generation rate is as great as the average execution rate.

Some macroinstructions return data to the host. Such data is returned from the cell array over either the direct memory access path or the GLOBAL line, either of which can be driven directly by any cell in the array. All data

Table 4.2 Conversion of the Macroinstruction ADD into Nanoinstructions.

A-address	B-address	Read-Flag	Write-Flag	MEM-ALU	Flag-ALU	Condition-Flag	Condition-Sense
2000	1000	Zero flag	1	A⊕B⊕F	AB+BC+AC	Zero flag	0
2001	1001	1	1	A⊕B⊕F	AB+BC+AC	Zero flag	0
2002	1002	1	1	A⊕B⊕F	AB+BC+AC	Zero flag	0
2003	1003	1	1	A⊕B⊕F	AB+BC+AC	Zero flag	0
2004	1004	1	1	A⊕B⊕F	AB+BC+AC	Zero flag	0
2005	1005	1	1	A⊕B⊕F	AB+BC+AC	Zero flag	0
2006	1006	1	1	A⊕B⊕F	AB+BC+AC	Zero flag	0
2007	1007	1	1	A⊕B⊕F	AB+BC+AC	Zero flag	0

returning to the host passes through the output FIFO. If the sequence of macroinstructions ever branches on the returning data, then the FIFOs must empty before the branch can take place.

4.6 Sample Operation: Addition

A typical macroinstruction sent from the host to the microcontroller is the ADD instruction, which specifies the addition of two contiguous variable length fields within each processor. In this section I show how this is converted by the microcontroller into nanoinstructions. The example is typical in its use of flags, memory, Arithmetic/Logic Unit operations, and iterations.

To execute an ADD macroinstruction, the host places four 16-bit integers into the input FIFO of the microcontroller. These integers specify, respectively, the op-code of the ADD instruction, the start-address of the source field, the start-address of the destination field, and the length of the fields to be added. The destination field is also used as a source.

Assume that the 8-bit number in memory locations 1000 through 1007 is to be added to the 8-bit number in locations 2000 through 2007, and that the carry-bit is to be left in flag 1. This operation is specified by the host by the instruction "ADD 2000, 1000, 8." This is converted by the microcontroller into the sequence of eight nanoinstructions shown in table 4.2.

Each bit in the source and destination is addressed in sequence, starting with the least significant bit. These two bits are added together with the flag bit taken from flag 1, where it was stored on the previous cycle. On the first cycle there is no incoming flag, so it is taken from the zero flag, which is always 0. The zero flag is also used for conditionalization, with a COND-sense of 0, because this operation is to be performed by all the processing elements.

The function for the memory is the exclusive-or function of the three inputs, which is 1 whenever an odd number of the inputs is 1, otherwise 0. The flag is the majority function of the three inputs and is 1 whenever two or more of the inputs are 1. This sequence of nanoinstructions can be generated by the microcontroller by means of a simple microcoded loop that increments the address of the memory locations.

Chapter 5

Data Structures for the Connection Machine

5.1 Active Data Structures

On a conventional computer, a data structure is a passive object. It is intended to be operated on, manipulated, and processed. On the Connection Machine data is stored in something that I call an *active data structure*. An active data structure is a machine. It is a special purpose processing device that is wired to operate on one particular piece of data and optimized for the operations it performs. The host controls the Connection Machine not by operating on the data, but by telling the data what to do. Because the structure must process as well as represent the data, data structures designed for the Connection Machine are different from those on a conventional computer. In this chapter I discuss various active data structures and give examples of what kinds of things they can do. I describe sets, trees, butterflies, strings, arrays, and graphs. Each of these has a natural representation on the Connection Machine in terms of cells connected by pointers. In addition, many of these data structures have a second representation that does not use pointers; instead, the connections between component cells of the data structure are implied by the addresses of the cells. This is called the *address-induced* representation of the data structure, connected by *virtual pointers*. Both normal and address-induced representations of various data structures are discussed in this chapter. Because they are active data structures, I show not only how they are represented but also what types of computations they can perform. In the final section I show how each of these structures corresponds to a type of xector.

5.2 Sets

Just as the simple, fundamental operations on a conventional computer involve operations on numbers, the fundamental operations on the Connection Machine involve sets. Set operations, such as union and intersection, are just as easy on the Connection Machine as the traditional unit-time operations of addition and subtraction are on a conventional computer. Just as the preferred iteration construct for serial computers is "for $i = 1$ to N," the most natural thing to do on the Connection Machine is to apply an operation to each member of a set. This is not to say that set operations cannot be formulated in terms of arithmetic or vice versa, but the easiest way of thinking about these things, the way that corresponds most closely to what is going on in the hardware, is different for the two types of computing machines.

When the Connection Machine deals with sets, it represents them as sets of processor/memory cells. The set is essentially the domain of a xector. The values of the xector, which might be edges of a graph, tuples of a relation, momenta of particles, or regions of an image, are stored in the memories of the cells. There are three different methods of explicitly representing such domain sets in the Connection Machine: bits, tags, and pointers. All three methods involve placing some form of marker on every member of the set, so that a cell's membership in the set is determined by the presence of the marker. Any normal set operation, such as intersection, union, labeling, or comparison, can be performed on any of the different representations of the set, although sometimes the operations involve converting from one form to another. The three set representation schemes (bits, tags, and pointers) are discussed separately in what follows.

5.3 Bit Representation of Sets

The simplest way to represent a set is to allocate one bit in every cell to indicate whether that cell is a member of the set. When cells are represented in this manner, the set operations correspond to simple Boolean operations applied to the corresponding bits in every cell. For example, assume that each member cell of set A is marked by a 1 in the ith bit of the cell's memory and that membership in set B is similarly indicated by the jth bit. Then we can form $C = A \cap B$ by having each cell store into the bit corresponding to C the logical AND of the ith and jth bit. In the same way the Boolean AND operation corresponds to intersection, OR corresponds to union, NOT corresponds to the complement, and so on. Because the Connection Machine can apply a Boolean operator to each cell simultaneously, these set operations take place in constant time, no matter how large the set. This bit-per-cell representation of a set is so easy to manipulate that other marking schemes are generally converted to the bit representation to perform these operations.

5.4 Tag Representation of Sets

One disadvantage of the bit-per-cell marking scheme is that representing a set requires allocating one bit in the memory of every cell in the machine, whether or not the cell is a member of the set. Because memory in each cell is limited, this is a significant disadvantage. One situation in which sets can be represented with greater memory efficiency is when a group of sets is known to be disjoint. An important example of this occurs when the sets of objects of different data types are stored. Because each object is of no more than one data type, the sets do not intersect. In cases like this it is advantageous to use a tag marking system.

Using bit labels, representing k sets requires k bits per cell. If we know that each cell is a member of no more than one of the k sets, then it is possible to represent all the sets using a total of $\lceil \log_2(k + 1) \rceil$ bits per cell. (The $+1$ covers the case in which a cell is not a member of any of the sets. If we know that each cell is a member of exactly one set, the sets can be represented with $\lceil \log_2 k \rceil$ bits per cell. In this case the k sets form a partition on the set of all cells. Because any set of disjoint sets can be turned into a partition by adding a "none of the above" set, I use this case as an example for the following discussion.

The $\lceil \log(k) \rceil$ bits in each cell are used to store a tag that indicates in which k set of the partition the cell belongs. $\log(k)$ bits are required so that there is a distinct tag for each k set. Because each cell belongs to exactly one set, storing a single tag is sufficient.

An important advantage of partitions is that within different portions of the partition, different storage conventions can be used to represent subpartitions or subsets of the partition. For example, assume that each cell represents an animal, a vegetable, a mineral, or nothing. The cells that represent animals can represent dogs, cats, people, kangaroos, warthogs, and lizards. Assume that the plants also partition into subcategories, say, seven of them. Minerals do not divide into subcategories but can belong to any combination of the following sets which can contain only minerals: soft, round, and red. Using the bit label representation would require $3 + 6 + 7 + 3 = 19$ bits per cell. By taking advantage of the hierarchy of disjoint sets, we can represent the sets by storing fields in each cell according to the following convention (this scheme uses a total of five bits per cell):

2 bits decoded as follows:

- 0 animals

- 1 vegetables

- 2 minerals

- 3 none of the above

3 bits decoded as follows:
   In animals:

- 0 dogs

- 1 cats

- 2 people

- 3 kangaroos

- 4 warthogs

- 5 lizards

   In plants:

- 0 trees

- 1 shrubs

- 2 grass

- 3 cacti

- 4 lichens

- 5 algae

- 6 mushrooms

- 7 halophiles

In minerals:

- the first bit indicates membership in SOFT

- the second bit indicates membership in ROUND

- the third bit indicates membership in RED

The example is contrived, but it is common in almost any program to divide objects into nonoverlapping "types" that have different storage conventions. The ability to take advantage of this in representing sets is important. In addition, the trick can be applied recursively so that subtypes use different storage conventions.

5.5   Pointer Representation of Sets

Neither the bit representation nor the tag representation is efficient when a set is small. This is because both schemes require the allocation of storage in every *potential* member of the set. If most of the potential members are not included, most of the storage will be wasted. A better way to store sparse sets in the Connection Machine is to connect all the members by pointers. This method of set representation was introduced in chapter 1 in the context of representing the graph. In the graph a balanced binary tree is used to represent the set of vertices connected by edges to a given vertex.

The normal way to represent a set by pointers is to choose one identified cell, the *root cell*, and to connect all members of the set to that cell by pointers. The pointers point from the root cell to the member cells. Because it is often not possible to store as many pointers in the cell as there are members of the set, the root cell normally points to a few *fanout cells*, which in turn can point to set members or to further fanout cells. As mentioned earlier, the depth of such a fanout tree, if it is kept balanced, is proportional to the logarithm of the number of leaves. In this case each leaf cell represents a member of the set.

One advantage of the pointer representation of a set over the bit and tag representations is that it is possible to store a pointer to the set by storing a pointer to the root cell. This capability is important when a set is to be included as a substructure of another data structure. For example, we can represent a set of sets by representing (with bits, tags, or pointers) the set of root cells of the member sets. Whenever I speak of a pointer to a set I mean a pointer to the root cell of a pointer-represented set.

To perform set operations on a pointer-represented set, we generally first convert the set to bit representation. This is accomplished by propagating a marker from the root cell through any fanout cells to the member cells. As will be seen, this kind of information spreading is one of the most important operations in the Connection Machine. It is another place where balanced fanout trees help. With fanout trees it is possible to mark a tree by marking each of the subtrees concurrently. This allows the entire set to be marked in a time proportional to the depth of the tree, that is, in logarithmic time. Marking all members of a set pointed to by a single node would require linear time. This can make the difference between 20 steps and a million. (I give a more detailed analysis of the time required to mark trees in section 5.8.)

Because set operations on pointer-represented sets involve converting to bit representation and because converting to bit representation requires logarithmic time, set operations on pointer-represented sets require logarithmic time. Performing the set operation itself requires only one single operation, for example, logical AND for intersection. This leaves the result in bit representation. If the result is required in pointer representation, it must be converted. This conversion of bit to pointer representation involves storage allocation and is discussed along with other storage allocating procedures in chapter 6.

The pointer method can also be used to represent ordered sets, or sequences. When representing a sequence, the two pointers pointing out from a fan cell are treated asymmetrically. The first one points to the items in the first half of the subsequence and the second to the second. This method of representing the order of a set requires no additional overhead.

5.6   Shared Subsets

The efficiencies of the various methods of representing pointer structures are discussed later in section 5.8, but, in general, the pointer representation of a set requires about $Ck \log N$ bits of storage for a set with k elements chosen from N potential elements, where C is a constant that depends on the details of implementation.

There are, however, situations in which the storage required to store multiple sets is much less than the sum of the storage of the individual sets. This is possible when the sets have common subsets. In this case the tree structure representing the common subsets needs to be stored only once. It can be shared among the supersets. This type of sharing is familiar to any Lisp programmer, and it has the same advantages and perils as shared list structures in Lisp. The primary disadvantage is that an operation that modifies the structure of one set affects other sets that share its structure. For example, inserting an item into one set can cause it to magically appear in another. While this effect can sometimes be used advantageously, it is generally considered undesirable.

There is also another problem with the use of shared tree structures that does not cause problems in Lisp. The depth of a balanced tree is the logarithm of the number of leaves. The depth of an extremely unbalanced tree, a linear list, for example, is about equal to the number of leaves. In Lisp the elements of a list are usually accessed in sequence; thus the total depth of the tree does not usually matter. In the Connection Machine, on the other hand, all the items are generally being accessed in parallel; thus the access takes a time proportional to the depth of the deepest item. In a well-balanced tree the depth is minimized because the deepest elements are essentially at the same level. This is why it is useful to keep trees balanced on the Connection Machine. Unfortunately, it is not always possible to keep trees reasonably balanced while sharing structure.

5.7   Trees

The most important Connection Machine data structure is the tree. Trees are used by themselves and as components of other data stuctures, such as graphs, arrays, and butterflies. We have already used them as a method of representing sets. Trees are useful because they provide a fast way of collecting, combining, and spreading information to and from the leaves. In this section I show algorithms on trees that add the leaves, count them, sort them, and number them. These algorithms all follow a pattern of recursion that is common in Connection Machine programming.

Trees are used to represent sets so that the leaf cells, the members of the set, can be reached quickly from the root. The short distance between root and leaves allows us to convert efficiently from pointer representation to bit representation by marking the root and recursively marking the subtrees until all the leaves are marked. This is an example of a *marker propagation* algorithm. Marker propagation is a common way to distribute data on the Connection Machine. In the set example the marker was a single bit, but it can also be a number or a pointer. Markers can also propagate simultaneously within multiple trees.

In addition to spreading information, it is often necessary to concentrate it. This requires pointers not only from the root to the leaves but also from the leaves to the root. These *back pointers* also pass through the fanout cells, so that in a binary tree no cell is pointed to by more than two others. This is important for the collection process. Imagine that we have a set of numbers at the leaves of a tree and that we would like the sum at the root. This can be accomplished by the spreading algorithm in reverse. (See figure 5.1.) Each leaf cell sends its number to the cell above, which adds the numbers from the left and right branches and sends up the sum. This is repeated until all the numbers are collected into a single sum at the root. Again, the algorithm takes a time proportional to the depth of the tree and can be performed on many trees simultaneously. Similar algorithms work with any associative two-place function, such as the associative Boolean functions (like AND and OR), multiplication, maximum, or minimum. One slight variation of this is to count the leaves of a tree by starting with each number as a 1 and then summing. Another variation is to check for equality of all the numbers by sending up from the left branch the message if both messages are equal and the special symbol FALSE if they are not. If the root sends any message other than FALSE, all items at the leaves of the tree are equal. This last algorithm works with any equivalence predicate.

The use of maximum and minimum in place of addition in the collection

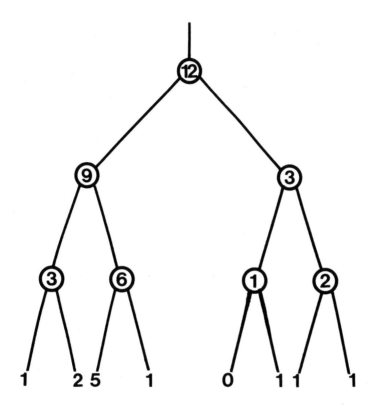

Figure 5.1 Computing the sum of the numbers at the leaves of a tree in logarithmic time.

algorithm gives an $N \log(N)$ time sort, where N is the number of leaves. Using the *max* operator, we can move the largest leaf to the top of the tree in $\log(N)$ time. The operation is then repeated with the largest element removed until all the elements are removed. Because this requires N cycles of $\log(N)$ steps each, the total running time is $N \log(N)$. This can be improved by a factor of almost $\log(N)$ by using a more complicated algorithm, because it is necessary to pay the $\log(N)$ transit time for the tree only once for the entire sort, rather than once for each element. This is accomplished by storing two elements at each node, one for each subtree, and sending up the greatest element as soon as there is room for it above. The root node accepts the items one by one in sorted order. In this algorithm a node with a free slot must indicate this to the corresponding node below, which then must send the data up. Therefore each step of the algorithm requires two communication steps. Because $\log(N)$ steps are required to fill the tree at the beginning, the entire procedure takes $2N + \log(N)$.

A faster version of the algorithm can be used when the order of the leaves can be predetermined. This is used, for example, to move the label of each of the leaves from left to right to the root of the tree. Each cell can keep a counter and can then send up an item at the appropriate time without the need for the signaling used in the sort. The number of communication steps in this method of generation is $N + \log N$.

Another logarithmic algorithm can be used to number the leaves of the tree from 0 to $N - 1$. The first phase is identical to the counting algorithm. This tells each node in the tree the number of leaves on the left and on the right. The second phase begins by sending a 0 to the root. When a node is sent a number, it sends the number to its left branch and the number plus the number of nodes in its left branch to its right branch. When a leaf receives a number, that is its number. This algorithm numbers the nodes from left to right, 0 to $N - 1$.

There are many more algorithms for trees (Browning 1980, Christman 1983). The ones discussed here are typical of the kinds that occur repeatedly in the Connection Machine. Notice that most run in logarithmic time. Because all logarithms on, say, a million cell machine, are less than 20, these algorithms are fast. They are sufficiently fast that they can be safely counted as constant-time operations when used as building blocks for more complex algorithms.

5.8   Optimal Fanout of Tree

There is no real reason to stick to binary trees. Trees with higher fanout
would use fewer nodes, and the distance between top and bottom would be
shorter. On the other hand, the nodes would need to be larger, and each
would have to handle more messages simultaneously. How do we trade off
these factors against one another? What is the optimal fanout? I consider
two different measures of optimality, minimal storage and minimal time.

First, let us consider what is optimal fanout for minimizing storage space.
It is easiest to calculate the optimal fanout for large trees, that is, trees with
arbitrarily many leaf nodes. Assume that the tree has N leaves for some large
N. We call a tree *balanced* if the sizes of the subtrees of every node differ
by no more than one and if all the subtrees are balanced. This definition
implies that only leaf nodes are unfilled. Let $S(N, k)$ be the number of cells
required to represent a balanced tree with N leaves and fanout k:

$$S(N, k) = \lceil \frac{N}{k} \rceil + \lceil \frac{N}{k^2} \rceil + \lceil \frac{N}{k^3} \rceil + \cdots + 1 \approx \frac{k^{\lceil \log_k N \rceil}}{k - 1}.$$

Each node has k entries each, so the total storage required to represent the
tree is $k \times S(N, k)$:

$$\text{Storage} = k \times S(N, k) \approx \frac{k^{\lceil \log_k N \rceil + 1}}{k - 1}.$$

The total storage is minimized when k is large; thus to minimize storage, we
must maximize fanout, at least in the case of large trees. This is fairly obvious
because there is overhead storage used in storing the internal structure of
the tree. Notice, however, that the storage penalty for using a nonoptimal
fanout is small. Even the simplest binary ($k = 2$) structure uses only twice
the storage of the optimal ($k = N$) large fanout node. So there is not much
to be gained by being optimal. This is especially true for small trees, in
which the overhead of keeping the tree balanced can be significant. For some
sizes of trees, a tree with a small fanout can actually require fewer nodes
than a tree with a slightly larger fanout. For example, a balanced tree with
eight leaves requires five nodes of fanout 4 but only three nodes of fanout
3. (See table 5.1.) If we take into account the increased storage required

for the larger nodes, the larger fanout becomes even less efficient. Unless the number of leaves is close to an even power of k, large nodes will waste storage. Table 5.1 shows the number of nodes in small balanced trees with various maximum fanouts.

Table 5.1 Choosing an Optimal Fanout. Memory Locations Required to Represent a Balanced Tree of N Nodes with Maximum Fanout k.

n	$k=2$	$k=3$	$k=4$	$k=8$	$k=16$
2	2	3	4	8	16
3	4	3	4	8	16
4	6	6	4	8	16
5	8	9	8	8	16
6	10	12	12	8	16
7	12	12	16	8	16
8	14	12	20	8	16
9	16	12	20	16	16
10	18	15	20	24	16
11	20	18	20	32	16
12	22	21	20	40	16
13	24	24	20	48	16
14	26	27	20	56	16
15	28	30	20	64	16
16	30	33	20	72	16
17	32	36	24	72	32
18	34	39	28	72	48
19	36	39	32	72	64
20	38	39	36	72	80
21	40	39	40	72	96
22	42	39	44	72	112
23	44	39	48	72	128
24	46	39	52	72	144
25	48	39	56	72	160
26	50	39	60	72	176
27	52	39	64	72	192
28	54	42	68	72	208
29	56	45	72	72	224
30	58	48	76	72	240
31	60	51	80	72	256
32	62	54	84	72	272

The second consideration in choosing a fanout is time. We wish to minimize the time required to operate a tree, for example, the time to send data from the root to every leaf. For the purpose of selecting the time-optimal fanout, I use a simple measure of time. Assume that each message requires exactly one time unit for transmission. During each unit time cycle, a node can send no more than one message. Any number of nodes can send a message simultaneously. When a node receives a message at the end of a time cycle, it can respond by sending a message at the beginning of the next cycle. Under these assumptions, the time required to make a large balanced tree, $T(N, k)$, is the depth of the tree times the fanout, minus a small correction for the unfilled nodes at the bottom of the tree:

$$T(N, k) = kx\lceil \log_k N \rceil - C\frac{dT(N, k)}{dk} = \log_k N \left(\frac{1}{\log_e k} - 1 \right).$$

The correction factor, C, is the maximum difference between k and the actual fanouts of the unfilled nodes in the bottom layer of the tree. Because C is necessarily less than k, it can be neglected for sufficiently large trees. The time cost is at a minimum for $k = e \approx 2.7$, the base of the natural logarithm. The closest integer is 3. As can be seen in table 5.2, both 2 and 4 are also good maximal fanouts for this simple measure of time.

In retrospect, 2 is actually not a bad choice for maximum fanout, although 3 is slightly better from a time standpoint, and 4 is better from a space standpoint. Because the time costs of 2-ary (binary) and 4-ary trees are essentially the same and because the 4-ary tree always requires fewer nodes, $k = 4$ is probably a better choice. In some special applications involving large trees, higher maximum fanouts may make sense.

Table 5.2   Choosing an Optimal Fanout Time (Time Required to Mark Leaves of Trees).

n	$k=2$	$k=3$	$k=4$	$k=8$	$k=16$
2	2	2	2	2	2
3	3	3	3	3	3
4	4	4	4	4	4
5	4	4	5	5	5
6	5	5	5	6	6
7	5	5	5	7	7
8	6	5	6	8	8
9	6	6	6	9	9
10	6	6	6	9	10
11	6	6	6	9	11
12	7	7	7	9	12
13	7	7	7	9	13
14	7	7	7	9	14
15	7	7	7	9	15
16	8	7	8	10	16
17	8	7	8	10	17
18	8	8	8	10	17
19	8	8	8	10	17
20	8	8	9	10	17
21	8	8	9	10	17
10^1	6	6	6	9	10
10^2	13	12	13	17	22
10^3	19	19	19	25	35
10^4	26	25	26	34	50

5.9   Butterflies

A single tree shrinks exponentially from the leaves to the root. This is fine for algorithms, such as the leaf scanning algorithm, in which the amount of data also shrinks exponentially toward the root. Many useful computations are not of this type. Sorting is an example. In sorting, all the input data must be in the output, so that the amount of data that must pass through each level is constant. The root of the tree becomes a bottleneck. We can fix this problem by using multiple trees that share the same leaves.

A structure that is built by sharing leaf nodes between two trees has as many nodes at the second level as at the leaves. This construction can be applied recursively to the two trees, such that the number of nodes at k levels remains constant through the use of 2^{k-1} trees. The resulting structure is called a *butterfly*. In a different context, discussed in chapter 2, a butterfly can also be called many other things, including an *omega network* and a *perfect shuffle*. The butterfly is familiar to many as the pattern of communication used in computing the Fast Fourier Transform (Cooley and Tukey 1965). (See figure 5.2.)

Because most of the cells in a butterfly are shared between multiple trees, the structure requires only $N \log N$ cells, or roughly $\log N/2$ times as many cells as a single binary tree. In some applications it is possible to reuse the same cells at each level so that each cell occurs $\log_2 N$ times in the structure. The version of the butterfly in which the same cells are used for each level is called a *Boolean n-cube*, for $n = \log_2 N$. This structure is isomorphic to an n-dimensional hypercube. We can therefore number the N corners of an $n = \log_2 N$ dimensional hypercube in a way such that the edges of the cube correspond directly to the links in the butterfly, with two numbers directly connected if and only if their n-bit binary representations differ by exactly one bit. Each number corresponds to the n-tuple of 1's and 0's that form the binary representation of the number. This n-tuple specifies the coordinates on the n-cube, with each dimension corresponding to one bit position.

This n-cube structure is useful when it is necessary to collect information at every node in a tree instead of just at the root. On the n-cube version, the N roots are identical with the N leaves. For example, if the leaf scanning algorithm is applied to a butterfly structure or to an n-cube instead of to a

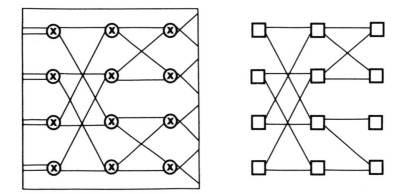

Figure 5.2 The butterfly pattern as used in the computation of a Fast Fourier
Transform.

tree, the sum will be generated at each of the N roots.

5.10   Sorting On A Butterfly

A butterfly structure with $N = 2^k$ leaf nodes is capable of sorting N numbers in a time proportional to k^2. For large N, this is considerably faster than the $N + k$ time required on the tree. The method described here, Batcher's bitonic sort (Batcher 1968), is based on repeated merging of successively larger sorted sequences.

A sequence of numbers is bitonic if it changes directions only once, that is, if it consists of a strictly nondecreasing subsequence followed by a strictly nonincreasing one, or vice versa. Batcher noticed that any bitonic sequence can be sorted by independently sorting the subsequences of odd elements and even elements, interleaving the results and then exchanging, if necessary, the first and second elements, the third and fourth, and so on. This works (roughly) because the bitonic property guarantees that selecting every other element gives a fair sample of large and small numbers. Interleaving the sorted subsequences results in a sorted sequence, except for a small sampling error that can be fixed by one exchange. Because any subsequence of a bitonic sequence is also bitonic, the method can be used to sort recursively the odd and even subsequences. The recursion stops at subsequences of length one, which are already sorted.

The pattern of comparisons in the bitonic sort fits well with the butterfly structure. During the ith step of the sort, elements j and k must be compared when $j = k \oplus 2^i$. These are exactly the pairs of elements that are connected in the butterfly at level i; thus each step of Batcher's bitonic sort requires exactly one communication step.

The bitonic sort can also be used repeatedly to sort arbitrary nonbitonic sequences. Appending any two sorted sequences results in a bitonic sequence, so that the bitonic sort can be used to combine two sorted sequences into a longer sorted sequence. This merge operation serves as a building block for a standard merge sort. Individual elements are merged into sorted pairs, pairs are merged into sorted groups of four, and so on until the entire sequence is merged into a single sorted group. Because each merge step takes time $\log_2 m$ to merge two lists of length m, the entire sort on N elements takes:

$$\sum_{m=1}^{\log_2 N} \log_2(2^m) = \sum_{m=1}^{\log_2 N} m \approx \frac{1}{2} \log^2 N.$$

5.11   Induced Trees

Because the structures of trees and butterflies are so regular, it is not always necessary to store the links explicitly. If the cells for the tree are allocated within a well-defined portion of the address space, it is often possible to calculate the structure of the tree or butterfly from the addresses of the cells. An important special case of this is when the tree spans the entire machine.

One method of inducing a tree, used on serial machines, is to connect cell i to cells $2i$ and $2i + 1$. This forms a tree on all cells from 1 to k. Because the addresses of the linked cells can be calculated, they need not be stored explicitly. Because these computed addresses can be used in the same ways as stored pointers, I call them *virtual pointers*. Induced structures are held together by virtual pointers just as normal structures are held together by stored pointers.

Figure 5.3 shows an example of an induced tree for $k = 3$. This method of address generation can be generalized to k-ary trees (Knuth 1968). For example, a ternary tree can be constructed by connecting cell i to cells $3i - 1$, $3i$, and $3i + 1$.

In the example, the induced tree is stored in memory locations 1 through 9. The tree could also be stored in any other contiguous k-long portion of address space by adding a constant displacement offset to the addresses. Butterfly structures can also be represented implicitly. Cells 0 through $n \log(n) - 1$ can be connected in an n-wide butterfly by connecting cell i to cells $i + n$ and $p(i) + n$, where

$$p(i) \;\; = \;\; i \oplus 2^{\lfloor \frac{i}{n} \rfloor})$$

A butterfly that shares the same cells at each level connects i to i and $p(i)$. Implicit binary butterflies also have r-ary equivalents.

Implicit trees and butterflies can be used with exactly the same algorithms as explicitly linked structures. The only difference is that instead of

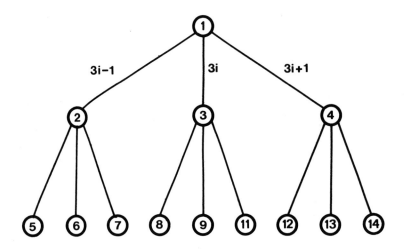

Figure 5.3 An induced 3-tree.

being stored, the pointers are computed. Because the computations necessary to compute the pointers are relatively simple, the additional overhead is not great.

Induced trees can be used to provide a secondary communications structure among cells that are also linked by explicit pointers. For instance, assume that we want to count all the cells in the machine with a certain property. If the cells were stored at the leaves of a tree, this could be accomplished in $\log_2 N$ time by the counting algorithm described earlier. If the cells are not explicitly stored in a tree, we can execute the algorithm anyway by using an induced structure. In this case, for example, we could use an induced butterfly structure with all the nodes used at each level. Each cell to be counted begins with a 1, the others with a 0. At each step each cell exchanges information with another, adding the incoming number to its total. On the ith step the cell exchanges with the cell $2i$ away. At the end of $\log_2 N$ steps, all cells have the full count.

This particular use of an induced structure, a shared butterfly ranging over the whole machine, is called *dimension projection* because it corresponds to projecting data across each dimension of a Boolean n-cube.

There is one information-gathering operation on induced trees that is so common that the Connection Machine provides special hardware to speed it up. This is the global OR operation, which is used to check if there is any cell in the machine that has a given property. This check can be performed by using a standard OR-to-root calculation on an induced tree covering the whole machine, but it is such a simple and common operation that it is worthwhile to support it in hardware. (This is called the *global tree* in the prototype). Even when the calculation is done in hardware, it takes logarithmic time, although the constant is smaller.

5.12   Strings

The factors that constrain computation on a Connection Machine are different from those on a conventional computer. Many of our assumptions about what is difficult and what is easy do not apply. This becomes clear in considering operations on one of the simplest of composite data structures, the *string*. The string is the address-induced version of the linear list. Instead of linking each element to the next, the ordered elements are stored in sequential locations in memory. The sequential allocation requirement limits the usefulness of strings in a conventional computer. For instance, inserting an element into a string requires moving all the elements in the rest of the string forward in memory. Space for the string to grow must be allocated in advance, and if strings are dynamically created and destroyed, allocation of contiguous memory segments becomes difficult. A common solution to these problems is to give up on strings and pay the price of storing a full linked list or to use some hybrid structure, such as CDR-coded lists or lists of strings. In practice, it is often necessary to use these more complicated data structures even when the algorithms are most naturally expressed as operations on strings.

On the Connection Machine it is possible to shift an arbitrarily large segment of data from one block of cells to another in unit time. Insertion into a string can be accomplished efficiently by shifting forward the entire contents of memory after the insertion point. If there are pointers to the object that moved, they have to be updated by adding a constant. This update can also be accomplished in unit time, assuming that the pointers are identifiable by something like a type code. For example, only the simplest text editors use this representation of memory on a serial machine because of the computational expense of inserting and deleting characters. The simplest data structure is rejected on the grounds of efficiency.

Searching strings is also fast. All occurrences of given substrings can be found in a time proportional to the length of the search string. Each cell in the string simultaneously checks to see if it matches the first item in the search string. If it matches, it activates the cell following it in the string. All activated cells then check to see if they match the second item in the search string. This process continues until all items in the search string are checked, at which point all activated cells mark the end's substrings that match the search string.

More generally, finding all occurrences of strings matching a regular expression takes a time proportional to either the maximum string satisfying the regular expression or the length of the searched string, whichever is shorter. The outline of the algorithm is that each element of the string simulates a finite state machine that recognizes the regular expression. At each step all elements pass their state to the next element forward, which performs the transition indicated by the stored symbol. This is repeated until either each finite state machine is in the reject or the accept state or until the last state is shifted to the end. Machines in the accept state mark matching substrings.

The ability to insert efficiently into even long strings makes possible some simple data structures that would be impractical on conventional machines. For example, in a text editor one obvious way to store the text is as a two-dimensional string, a string of strings. On a Connection Machine the simple way would also be efficient.

5.13   Arrays

Arrays are another type of address-induced data structure on the Connection Machine. Arrays can be any number of dimensions, but typically they are one or two dimensional. (The distinction here between a one-dimensional array and a string is how it is used. In a string we are generally interested in only the order of the elements. In an array we are interested in the absolute indexes.) Besides being particularly useful, one- and two-dimensional arrays fit well with existing implementation technology. Because integrated circuits and circuit boards are two dimensional, the communications network is likely to exhibit a two-dimensional locality that makes these patterns of communication particularly efficient. (This is the case on the prototype.) This locality is not critical for implementing arrays on the Connection Machine, but it is helpful in practice.

The comment regarding contiguous storage allocation for strings applies to arrays also. It is much easier to allocate contiguous blocks on a Connection Machine than on a conventional machine because arbitrarily large blocks of memory cells can be moved in constant time.

A typical application of arrays is in image processing in which a single cell is used to store the pixel at each point in the image. Here the two-dimensional structure of the array reflects the two-dimensional nature of the picture. Many image processing algorithms, particularly the lowest level signal processing steps, are linked directly to the two-dimensional structure of the image. For example, a typical image processing step is computing the convolution of an image with some filter. This is a weighted average of each pixel with its neighbors. For example, given the value of each pixel, $v(x, y)$, we might wish to compute the following quantity for each pixel:

$$V'(x, y) = \sum_{i=-r}^{r} \sum_{j=-r}^{r} C_{i,j} V(x + i, y + j).$$

This is called a *convolution* of radius r, where the $C_{i,j}$ terms are constants representing the function with which the image is being convolved. It is essentially a blurring step that filters out noise with spatial frequency less than r. It is a component step of many image processing computations.

Computing the Gaussian convolution of an image stored in a two-dimensional array on the Connection Machine in the most obvious way requires $4r^2$ steps, each involving a transfer, a multiplication, and an addition. This operation is performed on all pixels simultaneously so that the time required for the computation is independent of the size of the image.

To transfer the value $V(x+i, y+j)$ to the cell (x, y), each cell representing a pixel sends its value through the communications network to an address that differs from its own by some linear combination of i and j. Actually, the calculation of address is slightly more complicated than this because of special requirements at the boundaries of the array. If, for example, we are using periodic boundary conditions (wrapping), then the calculation of the address is

$$\text{address} = \text{base} + ((x + i) \text{ mod }_{\text{width}}) + ((y + j) \text{ mod }_{\text{height}} \times \text{width}).$$

Once the value is moved to the proper location it is multiplied by the appropriate constant and added to the accumulated total. Again, the multiplication and addition are performed simultaneously for every pixel in the image.

5.14 Matrices

Linear algebra provides one of the most concise notations for describing operations on large data structures. The language of vectors, arrays, and tensors is a powerful tool for representing concurrent algorithms because a single symbol can stand for an unlimited number of primitive operations.

$$\begin{bmatrix} 0 & 8 & 0 & 4 \\ 0 & 2 & 7 & 0 \\ 0 & 0 & 3 & 0 \\ 6 & 0 & 0 & 5 \end{bmatrix}$$

Figure 5.4 A small sparse matrix.

The operations are numeric in character, but they are often applicable to symbolic computations. Vectors can represent sets. Adjacency matrices can represent graphs. Multiplication by a matrix can give a permutation, and inversion can give a solution to a set of linear constraints.

Arrays are one way to represent matrices on the Connection Machine. Many of the comments given above regarding strings apply to arrays also. It is relatively easy to allocate contiguous storage for arrays dynamically because it is possible to shift concurrently memory and update pointers to displaced objects. In the array representation, multiplying an N-vector by an $N \times N$ matrix requires $2 \log_2 N$ communication steps, $\log_2 N$ addition steps, and one multiplication step.

A matrix can be multiplied by a vector represented by an array by using induced trees on the rows and columns of the matrix. The induced column trees are first used to distribute each vector component to all the array elements in the corresponding column ($\log N$ communication steps). All the multiplications of vector elements and array elements are then performed simultaneously. The leaf summing algorithm is then used to add the products in each row using the induced row trees ($\log N$ communication steps, $\log N$ addition steps). The resulting sum is for the product vector. Two $N \times N$ matrices can be multiplied, vector by vector, in $2N \log N$ time.

When a matrix is sparse, it can be faster and more storage efficient to represent the row and column trees explicitly. This is the pointer representation of an array. The trees contains all the information, so it is unnecessary to store the zero elements of the matrix. Figure 5.4 shows the tree representation of a small sparse matrix.

The array representation of an $N \times N$ matrix requires N^2 cells. The number of cells required in the tree representation depends on the number and distribution of the nonzero entries. If C_i is the number of entries in column i and R_j is the number of entries in row j, then the number of cells required to represent the $N \times N$ matrix with k nonzero elements using row and column trees is

$$\sum_{i=1}^{N}(C_i - 1) \; + \; \sum_{j=1}^{N}(R_j - 1) \; + \; k \; = \; 3k - 2N$$

because

$$\sum_{i=1}^{N} C_i \; = \; \sum_{j=1}^{N} R_j \; = k.$$

This is more storage efficient than the array representation whenever

$$k \; < \; N(N+2)/3.$$

The time required to multiply a vector can also be less. The time required to multiply a tree-represented matrix is

$$\max_{1 \leq i \leq N}(\lceil \log C_i \rceil) \; + \; \max_{1 \leq j \leq N}(\lceil \log R_j \rceil).$$

Because $C_i \leq N$ and $R_j \leq N$, this time will never be greater than $2 \log N$.

Matrix multiplication is a special case of a more general operation with the same spread-on-rows, collect-on-columns communications pattern. There is no need to always use the sum as the collection operation and the multiply to combine entries. This pattern of communication implements the more general inner product functions provided in the APL language.

5.15   Graphs

The most general active data structure on the Connection Machine is the *graph*. Graphs can be used to represent anything, including arrays, strings, and butterflies. As in most data structures on the Connection Machine, trees play an important role in the representation of graphs. Because graphs can be arbitrarily connected, there is generally no simple address-induced representation of a graph.

A graph can be represented by using a tree to represent each vertex. The leaves of the tree represent the edges leading into that vertex. If the

Table 5.3 Summary of Active Datatypes Described in Chapter 5.

Type representation	Pointer representation	Address-induced representation	Prototypical operation
set	Section 2.5	–	intersection
tree	Section 2.7	Section 2.10	sum to root
butterfly	Section 2.8	Section 2.10	sort
string	–	Section 2.11	search
array	Section 2.13	Section 2.12	image filtering
graph	Section 2.14	–	path-length

algorithm being used does not require any storage or computations on the edges, then the leaves of the trees of connected vertices can connect directly. That is, leaf cells in two trees can store pointers to each other. If the graph edge requires storage or computation then a cell is used to represent the edge and the connected vertex trees point to that cell. Notice that this representation of a graph is identical to the sparse matrix representation of the graph incidence matrix. This is not really surprising because these are only two different ways of viewing the same mathematical object. Figure 5.5 shows the representation of the graph whose incidence matrix is similar to the array shown in figure 5.4.

The path-length computation discussed in chapter 1 is an example of the kind of computation that can be performed with a graph. Many of the operations involve spreading and collecting data with the vertex trees. For instance, Step 3 of the path-length calculation involves each vertex calculating the minimum of its neighboring labels. This is accomplished by a two-step operation. First, each vertex spreads its label to the connecting edges. Next, each vertex uses the minimum function to combine the labels of connected vertices. Both operations use the vertex trees. Both are executed on all vertices simultaneously, so they take a time proportional to the depth of the deepest tree, that is, the logarithm of the degree of the most connected vertex. This is typical of operations on graphs.

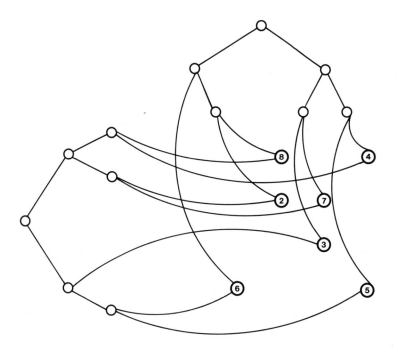

Figure 5.5 A graph with incidence matrix similar to array in figure 5.4.

5.16 Notes

Many of the algorithms in this text are based on serial algorithms. For good reviews see Knuth (1968) and Aho et al. (1974). The Fast Fourier Transform algorithm originally appeared in Cooley and Tukey (1965). For an even simpler explanation, see Bracewell (1984). For a discussion of induced structures and Connection Machine algorithms in general, see Christman (1983) and Bawden (1984).

Chapter 6

Storage Allocation

In this chapter I discuss how data structures on the Connection Machine are built. Because the machine is accessible to the host as ordinary memory, it is possible to build data structures by writing into the Connection Machine just as we would write into memory. This procedure works, but it takes place at the snail's pace of the serial host. The real question is: How during the course of executing concurrent algorithms can we build many data structures concurrently? How can a cell, or many cells, establish connections with unused storage and lay claim to it for building structures? How do we identify free storage? How do we reclaim storage that has been discarded? In Lisp jargon, how do we "cons" in parallel? These are questions that are answered in this chapter.

This is also the chapter in which we face the issue of how to handle defective cells, because the best mechanism for dealing with defects is to avoid building them into any data structures. This prevents them from being used in any computation. Normally, communications follow pre-established connections within data structures. If we do not build connections to defective cells when allocating storage, then there will be no communication with them.

I begin by ignoring the problem of defective cells and discuss various algorithms for allocating storage. Different algorithms are appropriate in different circumstances. I also ignore, at first, the problem of allocating contiguous blocks of storage for induced data structures. Instead, I concentrate on the problem of allocating single cells.

6.1 Free List Allocation

Before discussing methods for allocating storage in parallel, I discuss the method by which it is normally done serially. The algorithms discussed in this section can be executed directly from the host computer by treating the

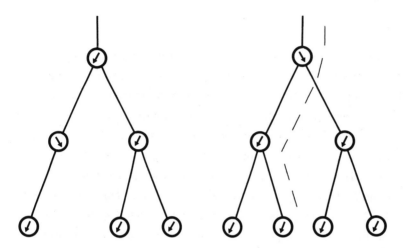

Figure 6.1 Balance bits allow new nodes to be added to a balanced tree.

Connection Machine as a memory. Because only one thing is being done at a time, the processing cells themselves need take no active part. The method of allocation I discuss is called *free list allocation*. It is essentially the same as that used in almost all implementations of Lisp and other languages in which resources are allocated from a "heap."

A free list is a linked data structure that contains all unused cells. The host keeps a pointer to the first cell in the list. That cell points to the next one and so on down the chain. The last cell has a special marker indicating that it is at the end of the chain. How the free list gets created is an interesting and important question and is discussed in later sections. Let us assume for the moment that some garbage collection process has identified all free storage and linked it together into a free list. To allocate a cell the host takes the cell from the front of the free list, to which it has a direct pointer, and updates its pointer to the next pointer in line. This cell can then be dealt into new structures by building pointers to it and modifying the pointers that it stores internally.

A common operation in the Connection Machine is to add a node to a tree such that the tree is kept well balanced. How do we decide where to add such a node? There is an elegant solution to this problem that involves adding one extra bit of bookkeeping information to each cell in the tree. I call this bit the *balance bit*. The balance bit is a 1 in a particular cell if the right subtree of that cell has one more node in it than the left subtree. If the left subtree has one more node or if the two subtrees are equal in size, then the balance bit is a 0. We need to consider only these cases because we are assuming that the tree is well balanced from the start and that the only problem of storage allocation is to keep it that way. The balance bits give the storage allocator directions as to where to add a new leaf. This works as follows. (See figure 6.1.) Starting from the root of the tree we go down to the left subtree if the balance bit is 1, and to the right subtree if it is 0. This causes us to move always toward the least populated subtree. As we pass through a cell, we toggle the balance bit, changing a 1 to a 0, and a 0 to a 1, so that the next time we go through, we reverse direction. When we reach a leaf, the new storage is allocated there. This algorithm can be extended to k-ary trees by using $\log k$ balance bits.

6.2   Random Allocation

The tree-balancing algorithm works for deciding where to allocate the storage in many trees simultaneously. Unfortunately, the free list indicates only one free node to be used at a time. Say that we want to add a new leaf to each of a thousand trees simultaneously. How can we do this? Assume that we have used the tree balancing algorithm on all the trees simultaneously to identify where to connect the newly allocated cells. Let us call this set of cells that would like to connect to free storage the *customers*. Let us also assume that some garbage collection process has marked all the potential free cells. The problem then is to get the customers and the free cells together.

The method that we use to accomplish this task depends on what percentage of the cells are free and what percentage of the cells are customers. Let us start with an easy case in which most of the cells are free and few of them are customers. In this case, if each customer chooses a random cell, it is likely to be free. If not, it can try again. Random in this case does not mean independently random for each cell. In fact, it is better if it is not independently random because it can avoid the problem of two customers trying to connect to the same cell. Instead, we generate one single global random number r. Each customer with address A tries to connect to the cell with address $A + r$. This guarantees that no two customers will try to connect to the same cell. If all the customers find a free cell at address $A = r$ then the goal is accomplished. If not, we repeat the process with the smaller set of unsatisfied customers using a new random number. How many times can we expect to repeat the process before all the customers are satisfied? Assume that each cell has a probability P of being free and that the number of customers is sufficiently small such that P is essentially the same before and after the allocation. In this case the probability that the cell has made a match after k trials is P (trials $\leq k$) = 1 - $(1 - P)^k$. If there are c customers, then the probability that all of the customers are satisfied after k trials, P (all $\leq k$) = $(1 - (1 - P)^k)^c$. The method works well when P is large. As an example, consider the case where $P = 90$ percent and $c = 100$ customers; then the probability that all customers are satisfied after four trials is greater than 99 percent. On the other hand, the method works poorly when P is small. For example, if $P = 10$ percent and $c = 100$ customers, then 88 trials are required to reach the same 99 percent confidence level.

The method has other disadvantages as well. Because a cell establishes a relationship with a completely random free cell, a complete stranger about which it knows nothing, it has no way of knowing whether the cell it is connecting to is defective. Another disadvantage of the scheme is that a cell has no tendency to connect to nearby storage. A customer can pass over a nearby free cell to connect to a randomly chosen one farther away. This has negative implications for the efficiency of communication in the network. Finally, this method of allocation is incompatible with free list allocation, so the host and the Connection Machine cannot both allocate storage without constantly rebuilding the free list.

6.3   Rendezvous Allocation

A method of storage allocation that fixes many of the bugs of random allocation is *rendezvous allocation* (Christman 1983). In rendezvous allocation free cells and customers are each assigned numbers. This number is then used to address a meeting place where the free cell and the customer make contact. This meeting place need not be a free cell so long as it has a little bit of extra storage to use for the rendezvous.

Rendezvous allocation depends on the fact that it is quick and easy to number the elements of a set. This is accomplished by modification of the leaf numbering algorithm, discussed in chapter 5, on the induced tree covering the whole machine. The algorithm works as follows. Every member of the set sends a 1 to the cell above it on the induced tree. This cell keeps track of the numbers that it receives from its left and right subtrees. It sends the sum of these two numbers to the cell above it on the tree. This process if repeated until the root is reached. At this point each cell has stored the number of members of the set that are in its left and right subtrees. The root of the tree then sends the number collected from its left subtree down to the root of its right subtree and sends a 0 down to the root of its left subtree. The process is then repeated by the root nodes of the two subtrees, except that, before the messages are sent, they add to them the number that they received from above. The process is repeated recursively until the leaf nodes themselves are sent numbers. At this point the n members of the set are given the numbers 0 through $n - 1$.

Rendezvous storage allocation can be accomplished by using this algorithm to number the free cells and by using it again to number the customers. These n numbers then serve as addresses for the rendezvous cells at which the customers and free cells meet. Each customer and free cell sends its own address to the cell specified by its number. This rendezvous cell cooperates by forwarding the address of the free cell to the address of the customer. The customer must then communicate with the free cell to inform it that it has been allocated and is no longer free. This completes the process of allocation.

Rendezvous allocation has an advantage over random allocation in that it continues to work well even when the number of free cells is small. In addition, if defective cells can be left out of the numbering process, then they can also be left out of the data structures. (There is a complication because of the possibility of defective rendezvous cells, but this can be fixed by using multiple rendezvous points.) The one problem that rendezvous allocation does not fix, however, is optimization of the locality of connections. There is nothing in the rendezvous scheme to ensure that a customer will make contact with the nearest free cell. This problem is fixed in the *wave allocation* scheme, described in section 6.4.

6.4 Waves

Wave allocation is a method by which a customer cell can find the nearest free cell. Unlike most Connection Machine algorithms, wave allocation depends on the physical topology of the communications network. This is because the locality that it is trying to preserve is a property of the physical topology. The purpose of trying to find free storage nearby is to reduce the load on the communications network. Wires are an expensive, and hence limited, resource. And the performance of the communications network is typically limited by the availability of free wires over which to send messages. If cells tend to communicate with nearby cells, messages will travel over fewer wires to reach their destination, and the total bandwidth of the network will be greater. Because storage allocation is the place where connections are established, this is a good place to optimize the locality of interconnection. (It is also possible to optimize interconnection locality post facto. This is discussed in section 6.8.)

To make the description of the wave algorithm easier, we assume that the topology of the communications network is a two-dimensional grid. This is probably not the case on any real network, but the algorithm that I describe has a counterpart for more complex topologies. We assume, at least for the purpose of the illustrations, that some nodes are farther away than others. If this is not the case, then the concept of locality makes no sense, and we might as well use another algorithm.

The wave allocation begins with each customer cell sending a request for free storage to its immediate physical neighbors. This request contains the return address of the customer. If the neighbor is free, it sends its own address in an acceptance message back to the customer. If it is not free, then it forwards the request onto its immediate physical neighbors. The expanding front of request messages propagates out from the customer like a wave. Hence the name *wave allocation*. Once the request wave makes contact with the free cell, an acceptance message is sent back immediately to the customer. This can happen at several points on the wave simultaneously. The customer accepts the first message and rejects the rest. It must now cancel its rapidly multiplying request for free cells. This is accomplished by sending out a "never mind" wave, which propagates at a faster rate than the request wave and cancels it when it catches up. The never mind wave contains the address of the free cell to which the customer has decided to link so that the other free cells that responded to the request can see that they were rejected.

This wave propagation process can take place for many customers at once. Because request waves contain the address of the originating customer, they each have their own identity. When two request waves collide, they must "stand off" until one of the waves is canceled. This guarantees that no two customers will try to connect to the same free storage location.

Wave allocation can avoid allocating defective cells so long as the neighbors of a defective cell know that it is defective. If this is the case, then they can refuse to communicate with it. They neither accept messages from it nor send messages to it. A request wave would never be propagated to such a cell; and even if it mistakenly felt that one was, its neighbors would refuse to forward it to the cell. This is among the most satisfactory of the defect tolerance schemes.

The primary disadvantage of wave allocation is that it is relatively slow because it involves sending many messages through the network. Deciding whether or not to use wave allocation is a trade-off between time spent during construction of storage and time spent on the activity of the active data structure.

There are many other algorithms for storage allocation. For example, there are parallel versions of the free list method that use a tree of free cells. There are also hybrid methods that combine waves and random allocation, free list and numbering, etc. Which method to use depends on the relative importance of factors such as speed, locality, and defect tolerance and on the statistical distribution of customers and free cells in the network.

6.5   Block Allocation

So far in the storage allocation algorithm we have dealt only with allocating single cells. For some data structures, for example, arrays, induced trees, and butterflies, it is necessary to have a contiguous segment of address space containing some number of cells. The algorithm described in this section is capable of allocating many such blocks concurrently, assuming that they are all of the same size. For the purpose of this algorithm we assume that the free storage contains the desirable number of blocks of contiguous free cells of the proper size. If this is not the case, then we may wish to rearrange the storage with a compaction operation such as the one described in section 6.7.

The idea is first to label every free cell with the number of contiguous free cells above, including itself. Let us assume that we are trying to allocate blocks of size k. Notice that every contiguous block of this size must have exactly one cell whose address is an exact multiple of k. We call this cell the *representative* of the block. The first phase of the algorithm results in the identification of all representatives of blocks of size k. The second phase of the algorithm involves linking these representatives with the customers. This second phase can be accomplished by either waves or rendezvous techniques. Identifying only the representatives is unique to block allocation.

The potential candidates for representatives are all cells whose addresses are 0 modulo k. All the candidates that are not free cells themselves can be eliminated immediately from consideration because they are obviously not a part of a free block of size k. We calculate for each of the remaining candidates two numbers. The first number says how many contiguous free cells there are directly below the candidate in address space. The second number says how many contiguous cells there are directly above it. If the sum of these two numbers is greater than or equal to k, we know that the candidate is indeed the representative of a block of the desired size.

The calculations of the lengths of the upward and downward contiguous blocks are carried out by similar methods. We consider here the calculation of only the upward block size. At the beginning of the algorithm we label each free cell with a 1 and each nonfree cell with a 0. For the first transmission step each cell sends its label to the cell whose address is one less than its own. If the cell that receives the message has a label of 0, that is, a label less than 1, it ignores the message. Otherwise, it adds the number in the message to its own label. On the next transmission step of the algorithm each cell sends its label to the cell whose address is two less than its own. If the receiving cell has a label that is less than 2, it ignores the message. Otherwise, it adds it to its own label. Next each cell sends its label to the cell whose address is four less than its own. And if the cell's label is less than 4, it ignores the message. This process repeats with each cell sending to the cell whose address is 2^i less than its own on the ith transmission step and each cell ignoring the message if its own label is less than 2^i, otherwise adding it to its own label. The process terminates when i is equal to the number of bits in the address of the machine. At this point, each cell has a label indicating how many contiguous free cells are directly above it in the address space.

This information can be used to choose a set of representatives. We choose as a representative every cell whose label is an exact multiple of the desired block size k. This cell represents the contiguous block of k cells starting with itself and moving upward in the address space. Because the label of each representative is a multiple of k, these blocks do not overlap. The representatives can then participate on behalf of their blocks in storage allocation in the same way that free cells participate in nonblocked storage allocation.

6.6   Garbage Collection

Up to this point we have assumed that all free storage cells are marked as such. The process of identifying and marking free storage is called *garbage collection*. (Occasionally a computer scientist will get nervous about writing a paper or working on a proposal having to do with garbage collection. In cases like this, the phrase *storage reclamation* tends to be used. It means the same thing.) Garbage collection can be and is done by ordinary serial machines. It is much faster and simpler on the Connection Machine. Deciding which cells are free is generally accomplished by eliminating all the cells that are used. A cell is used if it can be reached by following a chain of pointers from the host. There are basically three popular forms of garbage collection: reference counting, mark/sweep, and copying. All three have their corresponding algorithms on the Connection Machine.

The simplest form of garbage collection is *reference counting*. In a reference counting scheme, each cell keeps a count of the number of cells that are pointing to it. If this count ever goes to 0, then the cell is unused and becomes free. Reference counting is easy on the Connection Machine if a backpointer is stored for every pointer. If this convention is followed, then wherever there are pointers from a cell, there are pointers to it. A cell is free if and only if it contains no pointers. Although this is simple in practice, consistently maintaining this discipline of always storing backpointers is cumbersome. It also needs to be complicated if the implied pointers of induced structures are taken into account. Besides being cumbersome, reference counting garbage collection has a fatal flaw. It is possible to build circular structures that point to themselves and yet are pointed to by nothing else. The simplest case of this is a cell that simply points to itself. In a strict reference counting scheme these structures are never identified as free storage.

Perhaps the most popular garbage collection scheme is called *mark/sweep*. This is a two-phase algorithm. The first phase marks all used storage and the second links together all unused storage into a free list. Depending on which storage allocation scheme we are using, we may be interested in both phases of this algorithm or in only the first. The mark phase is essentially a marker propagation starting at known objects and following all possible pointers. For the purpose of describing this and other garbage collection algorithms, we assume, without loss of generality, that there is only one known object, a master data structure that includes pointers to all others. Such a master structure is often called the oblist in Lisp implementations. It is important that this oblist contains pointers to all useful storage except the free list, and that it does not contain a pointer to the free list. Anything not pointed to directly or indirectly by the oblist is considered unused "garbage." The mark phase of garbage collection works as follows. A mark is placed on the oblist. All marked cells then send messages to mark each of the objects to which they point. This step is repeated until no new cells are marked, at which point the mark phase is completed and all unmarked cells can be considered free storage. Notice that it is difficult for this algorithm to follow implied pointers within induced structures. For this reason, induced structures are generally sewn together with a tree of pointers when they are created. These pointers serve no use except to mark the structure against garbage collection.

If it is desirable to form a free list of the unmarked cells, this can be accomplished by using the induced tree on all the elements to form free cells into a linked list. Every unmarked cell sends its address up toward the root of the tree. If a cell receives two pointers, it sends the pointer from the left branch to the cell pointed to by the right branch. Then it sends the pointer from the right branch up the tree. If a cell receives only one pointer, it sends it up the tree. A cell can determine that it is to receive only one pointer either by depending on the balance of the tree or by using a "no pointer" message initiated by the marked cells and propagated by any cell receiving two "no pointers." Each time an unmarked cell receives a pointer as a message, it stores it, establishing a link to that cell. This process of sending upward and linking is repeated until the root node sends up a pointer, in which case that is the pointer to a linked list of all the free cells.

The mark phase of this garbage collection algorithm takes place in a time proportional to the maximum depth of any structure pointed to by the oblist. If all the structures form a reasonably well-balanced tree, then the maximum depth is of the order of the number of address bits in the machine, or less if much of the storage is unused.

6.7 Compaction

The mark/sweep garbage collector rearranges connections among only the free cells; it leaves existing structures intact. It is sometimes desirable to rearrange existing structures either to shorten communication distances or to create large contiguous blocks of storage. This can be achieved, for example, by moving all data structures into a contiguous block at the beginning of memory and leaving the entire upper portion of the address space full of free cells. A garbage collector that accomplishes this is called a *compacting* garbage collector.

Any compacting garbage collector must perform two tasks. First, it must move existing structures into a contiguous area of memory. And, second, it must update pointers between existing structures so that they point to the structure's new location. The second task is generally harder than the first. Before describing how the compacting garbage collection algorithm works, let me digress and describe an important subroutine, namely, finding the minimal spanning tree of a graph.

Any graph has a subgraph without cycles that includes all its vertices. This acyclic graph is called a spanning tree. It is not difficult to find some spanning tree within a graph. It is more difficult, and often impossible, to find a balanced spanning tree, particularly if we insist on finding the tree rooted at a particular vertex. The algorithm that follows finds such a balanced tree if one exists. In any case, it finds a spanning tree of minimal depth, that is, with minimal distance from the root to the farthest leaf. It works by building up a tree from the root and by adding repeatedly all connecting edges that do not form cycles.

Given a graph G and a root vertex v, we wish to find an acyclic subgraph T of G connecting all vertices of G such that the maximum distance of any node in T to v is minimized. We begin with the set of vertices of T, V_T, initially containing only V, and the set of edges E_T, equal to $\emptyset$. We begin by marking every edge connecting to a vertex in V_T. For every vertex not in V_T, if it connects to one or more marked edges, we add the vertex to V_T and choose one of the marked edges to add to V_E. This process is repeated until all the vertices of G are in V_T.

So long as G is connected, the execution of the algorithm above clearly yields a subgraph of G that connects all the vertices. It contains no cycles because adding a new vertex to a graph and a single edge connecting that vertex can never create a cycle. And this is the only way that the algorithm can add edges. We can prove that it is of minimum depth by contradiction. Assume that there is some sequence of edges E that connects vertex v_1 to the root vertex v in fewer steps than those used to connect v_1 and v in T. Then there must be some edge e in E but not in T that connects directly a vertex v_E of distance D from v to T and a vertex v_E at a distance greater than $D + 1$. If this were not the case, then the path from the root to T would be as short as E. But any such edge would have to be marked on the deep step of the algorithm and would be part of T unless v_E was already in T or there would be another edge added adjoining v_E. In either case, v_E would be connected in T at a distance not greater than $D + 1$, which is a contradiction. Therefore no vertex is farther from v in T than it is in any other subgraph of G, including G itself.

The simplest way to compact the data is to label each cell with the number of free cells that have smaller addresses than it does. This can be accomplished in logarithmic time by a variant of the counting algorithm. Once all cells are labeled in this manner, the label can serve as an offset. Each cell calculates its new address by subtracting the label from its current address. Each cell then copies itself by sending messages to the new address, leaving behind a forwarding pointer (we are assuming here that there is enough working storage within a cell to do this). The forwarding pointer is used in the pointer updating process. This is accomplished by each cell sending a message to every cell that it points to asking for the forwarding address. These forwarding addresses are used to replace the pointers to the old objects. Once this process has been completed, the old objects no longer need to store the forwarding addresses. Notice that this method of compaction leaves contiguous blocks of storage contiguous.

6.8   Swapping

Data structures that have been compacted in the lower portion of address space exhibit better locality than those that have not, but they still may be far from optimal. If backpointer structures are kept, that is, if a cell points to all cells that point to it, then a cell can move itself so long as it informs its acquaintances of its new address. This allows two cells to exchange places to optimize locality. This process is called *swapping*.

To decide when to swap, a cell communicates with each of its immediate physical neighbors. They exchange information about which direction, if any, they would like to move and on this basis decide whether it would be to their mutual benefit to swap places. In general, a cell would like to move in a particular direction if it would shorten its average communication time. How this is measured depends on the details of the communications network. On a Boolean n-cube network, for example, a good approximate measure of communication difficulty for a cell is the sum of the Hamming distances to the communicating cells. The cell would like to move, that is, change its address, in a direction that decreases that number. A simple situation in

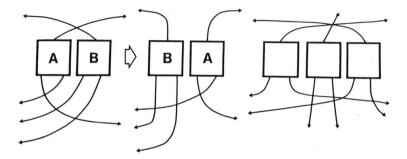

Figure 6.2 Data structures can exchange positions in order to shorten communications distances.

which it is to the benefit of both cells to swap is shown on the lefthand side of figure 6.2.

If cells swap only when it is to their mutual benefit, then the optimization process will quickly get stuck at a local optimum. Figure 6.2 shows (on the righthand side) such a stuck case in which the middle cell is happy where it is and refuses to budge. This prevents the cells on either side from exchanging places. There are several possible solutions to this problem. One of the most elegant is called *simulated annealing* (Kirkpatrick et al. 1983). In simulated annealing we sometimes swap two cells even when it is not to their mutual benefit. The probability of making such an exchange is a decreasing function of time. This gradual reduction of randomness to find the optimal network is analogous to gradually reducing the heat while growing a crystal, hence the name "simulated annealing." In fact, the analogy can be made precise by the following formula:

$$P(\Delta E) =_e \frac{-\Delta E}{KT}.$$

Here P is the probability of making a nonoptimal exchange, T is the simulated temperature, K is the Boltzman constant, and ΔE is a measure of the cost of the change. This method of simulating annealing is known as the *Metropolis algorithm* (Metropolis et al. 1953). To do it really right, we should make only one change at a time because the ΔE terms are not strictly local.

Another more practical approach is to move only some subset of the cells at a time and to choose the subsets such that no connected cells are in the same subsets. Such a collection of subsets is called a *coloring* of the graph of connected cells, and good heuristics exist for generating good colorings, many of which are suitable for parallel implementation.

Swapping to optimize locality cannot conveniently be done concurrently with other computations. It is best done while nothing else is going on. Because it performs an optional optimization, perhaps the best time to do it is while the machine is otherwise idle. This allows the machine to dream usefully while the user decides what question to ask next.

6.9   Virtual Cells

Up to this point we have assumed that there are enough cells in the Connection Machine to hold the entire problem. Of course, there will always be problems too big to hold on a physical machine. This problem comes up in conventional computers with the size of memory. The memory problem has been alleviated to some extent through the use of virtual memory, which allows programs to be written as if physical memory were much larger than it is. This is accomplished by actually storing the data in some secondary storage device and bringing it into memory only when it is actually used. Can a similar technique be used to provide *virtual cells* on the Connection Machine?

The biggest technical obstacle in building a virtual Connection Machine is doing something sensible when a real cell sends a message to a virtual cell that has been "swapped out" into secondary storage. There are essentially two ways to deal with this problem. One is to bring the cell back into physical address space. The other is to save the message.

6.10   Notes

For a discussion of simulated annealing, see Kirkpatrick et al. (1983) and White (1984) (a detailed practical analysis). The Metropolis criterion comes

from Metropolis et al. (1953). The enumeration consing algorithms are
based on those given in Christman (1983). Tom Knight first suggested the
swapping method of optimizing storage in the Connection Machine.

The classic works in fault tolerance are Moore and Shannon (1956) and
von Neumann (1956). For a discussion of error correcting codes, see Peterson
(1972) and Bobrow and Arbib (1974). For a specific analysis of fault tolerance
and two-dimensional grids, see Manning (1975).

Chapter 7

New Computer Architectures and Their Relationship to Physics or, Why Computer Science is No Good

> "It is therefore quite possible that we are not too far from the limits which can be achieved in artificial automata without really fundamental insights into a theory information, although one should be very careful with such statements because they can sound awfully silly in five years."
>
> — John von Neumann, 1949

Will we ever have a model of computation that is as powerful and beautiful as our models of physics? In this final chapter I argue that the development of such a model will be the direct consequence of the development of a new wave of computer architectures like the Connection Machine. The chapter is divided into three parts. In the first I point out that computer science is missing many of the qualities that make the laws of physics so powerful: locality, symmetry, invariance of scale. This is why physics is so nice and computer science is not. In the second section I give an example of physicslike laws that occur in a Connection Machine. In the final section I give some reasons for expecting more of this convergence of physical and computational law in the future.

7.1 Why Computer Science is No Good

In the past, computer scientists have found it convenient and productive bto adopt a model of the computational universe that is different from our models of the physical universe. This is changing. As we build bigger computers out of smaller components, our models of computation are forced to change. There is reason to hope that our new models for specific systems will be similar to the models of physics.

A computer designer is constrained by mundane problems that have no counterparts in the theoretical models of computer science: the size of connectors, the cost and availability of components, the mechanical layout of the system. Recently these factors have dictated a dramatic change in the way we design computers. Things don't look the same. Wires cost more than gates, software costs more than memory, and the air conditioner takes up more room than the computer. Our current models of computation are inadequate for designing or even describing our new architectures. An abstract model is powerful only when it allows us to pay attention to certain aspects of a situation while ignoring others. Our current models seem to emphasize the wrong details.

The areas in which computational models are weak are often the areas in which they differ from physical models. In physics, for example, many fundamental quantities are conserved, whereas in our old models of computation, data can be created or destroyed at no cost. This is a difference and a weak point. The big air conditioner sitting next to the small computer is testimony to this fact. Other differences in physical and computational models also seem to cause problems. I point to only one sort of difference here, the difference in locality, although similar arguments can be made for symmetry, linearity, or continuity.

In the physical universe the effect that one event has on another tends to decrease with the distance in time or in space between them. This allows us to study the motions of the Jovian moons without taking into account the motion of Mercury. It is fundamental to the twin concepts of *object* and *action*. Locality of action shows itself in the finite speed of light, in the inverse square law of fields, and in macroscopic statistical effects, such as rates of reaction and the speed of sound. In computation, or at least in our old models of computation, an arbitrarily small event can and often does cause an arbitrarily large effect. A tiny program can clear all of memory. A single instruction can stop the machine. In computation there is no analog of distance. One memory location is as easily influenced as another.

Fundamental to our old conception of computation was the idealized connection, the wire. A wire, as we once imagined it, was a marvelous thing. You put in data at one end and simultaneously it appears at any number of useful places throughout the machine. Wires are cheap, take up little room, and do not dissipate any power.

Lately, we have become less enamored of wires. As switching components become smaller and less expensive, we begin to notice that most of our costs are in wires, most of our space is filled with wires, and most of our time is spent transmitting from one end of the wire to the other. We are discovering that it previously appeared as if we could connect a wire to as many places as we wanted, only because we did not yet want to connect to many places. We have been forced to notice that we cannot measure a signal without disturbing it; for example, we must drive a wire with power proportional to the number of inputs that sense it. Of course we knew this before, but the fact seems more significant when the number in question is ten million instead of just ten. Also, real wires take up room. Because we are building in mere three-dimensional space, it is impractical to connect components arbitrarily. When we were wiring up a few hundred vacuum tubes, this was not a problem, but today we need to wire together hundreds of millions of components, and we need to do it in a smaller space. Most of the wires must be short. There is no room for anything else. (There are also similar problems with memory locations, which are just wires turned sideways in time.)

Our models of computation do not offer much help in solving the problem. Until recently, they abstracted the wire away into a costless and volumeless idealized connection. Our old models impose no locality of connection, even though the real world does. This is a prime example of where our old models break down. (In classical computation the wire is not even considered. In current engineering it may be the most important thing. Something is wrong with the theory.)

7.2 Connection Machine Physics

Consider a Connection Machine with a two-dimensional communications network, as illustrated in figure 7.1. A message is addressed to the appropriate cell by specifying the relative displacement in the grid of the recipient from the sender (for example, up two and over five). This does not specify the route the message is to take, just its destination. The sender mails a message

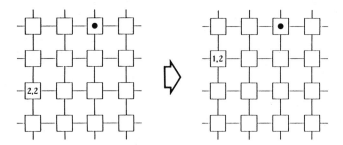

Figure 7.1 A message moving toward its destination in a two-dimensional communications network.

by handing it to a neighbor, and the neighbor decides on the basis of the address which way to send the message next. If the y displacement is positive, it will go up. If the x displacement is negative, it will go left. The neighbor modifies the address by incrementing or decrementing it appropriately, so that when the message reaches its intended destination, both displacements are zero. For example, a communicator receiving a message addressed "two up and five over" can change it to "one up and five over" and send the message to the communicator above.

Delivering messages takes time, so the distance between communicating cells is important. The metric is not the same as in Euclidean space because there are no diagonals. The taxicab metric $(\Delta x + \Delta y)$ is closer, but even this needs some refinement. The problem is that each cell has only a finite number of states, so it can only handle a few messages at one time. Messages may need to sidestep congestion. It is no problem to design local routing algorithms that will accomplish this, but the effective distance between two objects is increased. We need a metric that takes this into account.

We define the distance between two points as the average communication time between them. In an empty cellular space this is the same as the taxicab metric. The presence of an an intervening object distorts the metric because messages must flow around it. The curvature of the optimum message paths (geodesics) increases with the density of objects. The farther away the objects, the less the effect, so there is a local distortion in the metric proportional to the density of objects.

This distortion is not quite the same as physical gravity, and I do not suggest that the causes of the two are similar, but it is interesting to find an effect in computation that is so similar in form to one in physics.

Here is another one. Imagine that two cells are sitting next to each other in the grid. Imagine that the left cell communicates mostly with cells off to the right and that the right cell communicates with cells to the left. It would be advantageous (in the sense of minimizing communication time) if the cells were to exchange places, bringing each of them nearer to the cells with which they communicate. The hardware of the cell cannot move, but two cells can exchange their internal states. The effect is the same. The computation object that was in the right cell moves to the left cell, and vice versa. (Interested parties must be informed of the change of address, but this turns out to be easy on the Connection Machine.)

By this mechanism, with some refinements, the hardware of the machine causes each cell to migrate in the direction in which it sends most of its messages. Groups of intercommunicating cells tend to cluster. In such a system paths of communication act like attractive forces that bind the cells together. On a larger scale the clusters act like objects. They have strong internal forces and weaker interactions with other objects. Communication between two clusters tends to pull them together. This motion is a cumulative effect of the local behavior of the individual cells, but it can be analyzed as a macroforce between two objects. There is no need to pay attention to the detailed interactions of the individual cells.

We could give specific local rules that cause the macroforces to behave like $F = Ma$, but that would miss the point. The point is not that this is a good model of physics (it isn't), but that the laws that describe its behavior are similar in form to physical laws. Remember that the purpose of the machine has nothing to do with physics. It was designed the way it was for good, hard engineering reasons: the cost of connectors, the need to dissipate heat, the volume of wires. Any similarity to physics, living or dead, is purely unintentional, but not coincidental.

7.3   New Hope for a Science of Computation

Progress in physics comes by taking things apart; in computation, by putting things together. We might have had an analytic science of computation, but as it worked out, we learned more from putting together thermostats and computers than we did from taking apart monkey brains and frog eyes. The science of computation, such as it is, is synthetic.

The respective models of physics and computation reflect the difference in approach. For example, in classical physics most quantities are continuous. As physicists probe deeper into lower and more fundamental levels of reality, things begin to look discrete. The physicist of yesterday measured. The physicist of today counts. In computation things are reversed. We have begun in the other direction and, because we have begun only recently, we have not gone far. This is one of the reasons that computer science seems to be "no good": We have not gotten beyond counting. Knowing the lowest level rules is good, but it is in no way sufficient. Quantum chromodynamics is not much use in designing bridges. (Computer science is not much use in designing computers.)

I am not discouraged. While physics is looking down into lower and lower levels, computer science is looking up. It is looking up because systems are becoming large enough to exhibit the kind of simple, continuous behavior that we are accustomed to in everyday physics, large enough that the behavior of the system can no longer be dominated by the behavior of any single component. There is beginning to be a forest to see through the trees.

There are two sorts of things that could be called computational models, and I would like to make clear which one I am talking about. By computational model I could mean a model of all possible computational worlds. There have been a few important steps toward such a metacomputational theory (theories of servomechanisms, Turing computability, information theory), but so far a complete and coherent model is still beyond sight. The second sense of computational model is a model of a particular computational system. Physics may be such a model. Physical law does not need to describe what might happen in any possible universe, just this one. In computation the distinction is more important because we design our own worlds. The Connection Machine is an example of such a world.

We see no way to predict the development of a generalized theory of computation, but we do see reasons to expect good, clean, useful models of specific computational systems — models that will look like physics. The first reason is that physical law itself seems to be such a model. If the universe is a computing machine, then we know that at least some computing machines have elegant laws. This view of the universe is well represented elsewhere (Landauer 1967, Toffoli 1977, Wolfram 1984a), and I will not dwell upon it.

The second reason for believing in physical/computational model convergence is more profound and therefore more likely to be wrong. Both sciences study large systems of weakly interacting components. Such systems, with local rules of interaction, often seem to have simple macrolaws. This may be due to some "law of large systems" corresponding to the central limit theorem in statistics. The theorem says that the sum of many random variables always has a simple Gaussian distribution, whatever the distributions of the variables. A sum represents less information than its addends, and the Gaussian distribution has minimum information. In the same way, when we add together the individual behaviors of components, we lose information. Only the simple linear properties show through. Classical physics is simple because only simple additive properties, like momentum, remain visible at the macroscale.

The final reason for expecting physicslike behavior in computational systems is that all our computing machines must be implemented in the physical world. As our components become smaller and more efficient, they must inherit some of the constraints of the physical laws. Machines will have three-dimensional connectivity because space is three-dimensional. They will have limited propagation rates because space has a finite speed of light. As less is wasted between function and implementation, the physics begins to show through.

These conjectures will be tested because in the future we will be building even larger computing machines out of even smaller components. Perhaps we will grow crystals with each lattice site pointing to a processor. What will computation look like with a mole of processors? Much like physics, I think. When this happens, we can look ahead to new models of computation, models that may inherit some of the power and the beauty of physical law.

7.4   Notes

The text of this chapter was adapted from Hillis (1982). It appears in one of three special volumes of the *International Journal of Theoretical Physics* that deal with physics and computation. Most of the papers in these volumes are related to the subjects discussed in this chapter and the complementary subject of using computational models to describe physics, as in Landauer (1967) and Toffoli (1977). The von Neumann quote is from von Neumann (1949).

Annotated Bibliography

Abelson, Harold, and Peter Andreae (1980). "Information Transfer and Area-Time Tradeoffs for VLSI Multiplication," Integrated Circuit Memo 80-4, Department of Electrical Engineering and Computer Science, Massachusetts Institute of Technology. (A good example of the use of information transfer models to bound the difficulty of a computation. See Thompson (1979).)

Aho, V.A., J.E. Hopcroft, and J.D. Ullman (1974). *The Design and Analysis of Computer Algorithms*, Addison-Wesley. (The standard introductory text. See also Knuth (1968).)

Anderson, John R. (1983). "Retrieval of Information from Long-Term Memory," *Science*, April 1983. (Talks about spreading actuation memory retrieval. Gives evidence that access time goes up with fanout.)

Applegate, James H., Michael R. Douglas, Yekta Gursel, Peter Hunter, Charles L. Seitz, and Gerald Jay Sussman (1985). "A Digital Orrery," *IEEE Transactions on Computing* (A special purpose computer for simulating planetary motions. Has ten processors, one for each planet and one for the sun.)

Aristotle, *Politics*, translated by Ernest Barker (1946). Oxford University Press, Oxford, England. (The section on "slavery" contains the first written reference, of which I am aware, to thinking machines.)

Arvind, K. P. Gostelow, and W. E. Plouffe (1978). "An Asynchronous Programming Language and Computing Machine," TR114A, Department of Information and Computer Science, University of California at Irvine. (Describes the Irvine Dataflow language.)

Arvind, D. E. Culler, R. A. Iannucci, V. Kathail, K. Pingali, and R.E. Thomas (1983). "The Tagged Token Data Flow Architecture," Massachusetts Institute of Technology, Laboratory for Computer Science Memo 229. (Describes a tagged data flow architecture. See also Dennis (1980).)

Ashby, W. Ross (1956). "Design for an Intelligence-Amplifier," in *Automata Studies*, C. E. Shannon and J. McCarthy (eds.), Princeton University Press, Princeton, NJ. (An optimistic prediction for the near-term prospect of AI, or rather, cybernetics.)

Backus, J. (1978). "Can Programming be Liberated from the von Neumann Style?" *Communication of the ACM* (8): 613–641. (A classic. Introduces the phrase "von Neumann bottleneck," and "FP," an applicative programming language that has some relation to CmLisp.)

Bartlett, F. C. (1932). *Remembering: A Study in Experimental and Social Psychology*, Cambridge University Press. (Competitive analysis. Performance measurements of human memory.)

Batcher, K. E. (1968). "Sorting Networks and their Applications," *Spring Joint Computer Conference*, 307–314. (Batcher is the original sorting network hacker.)

Batcher, K. E. (1974). "STARAN Parallel Processor System Hardware," *AFIPS Conf. Proc.* 43: 405–410. (STARAN was one of the first fine-grained parallel processors ever built. See also Surprise (1981).)

Batcher, Kenneth E. (1980). "Design of a Massively Parallel Processor," *IEEE Transactions on Computers*, C-29 (9). (A good overview of the MPP, which is like the Connection Machine, without the connections.)

Bawden, Alan (1984). "A Programming Language for Massively Parallel Computers," Master's Thesis, Massachusetts Institute of Technology. (Describes CGL, Connection Machine Graph Language, a high-level language for the Connection Machine that is a much more radical departure from conventional programming languages than CmLisp.)

Bawden, Alan and Philip E. Agre (1984). "What a Parallel Programming Language Has to Let You Say," AI Memo 796, Massachusetts Institute of Technology, Artificial Intelligence Laboratory. (One of the first efforts to develop a high-level language for the Connection Machine.)

Bell, C. Gordon (1985). "Multis: A New Class of Multiprocessor Computers," *Science* 228: 462–467. (A good review of multicomputers, past, present and future.)

Benes, V. E. (1965). *Mathematical Theory of Connecting Networks and Telephone Traffic*, Academic Press. (The standard text for telephone switching system. Describes Benes Networks and Clos Networks. Very readable.)

Berman, Oded, and Richard C. Larson (1982). "The Median Problem with Congestion," *Computers & Operations Research* 9 (2): 119–126. (Shows a solution to the problem of locating servers to minimize travel time given server congestion.)

Bernstein, P. A. and D. W. Chiu (1981). "Using Semi-Joins to Solve Relational Queries," *Journal of the Association for Computing Machines* 28 (1): 0025–40. (Shows that tree queries are easy, but cyclic ones are probably hard.)

Bhatt, Sandeep Nautum (1981). "On Concentration and Connection Networks," MIT-LCS-TM-196. (An $O(n)$ construction of concentrator and 795 $n \log(n) + o(n)$ construction of connector.)

Bobrow, Leonard S., and Michael A. Arbib (1974). *Discrete Mathematics: Applied Algebra for Computer and Information Science*, W. B. Saunders Company. (Contains a good introduction to error correcting codes.)

Bobrow, Daniel, and Allen M. Collins (eds.) (1975). *Representation and Understanding: Studies in Cognitive Science*, Academic Press.

Boden, Margaret (1977). *Artificial Intelligence and Natural Man*, Basic Books. (A history of the development of AI.)

Bolt Beranek and Newman Inc (1985). "Development of a Butterfly Multiprocessor Test Bed," Rep. 5872, Quarterly Technical Report No. 1. (A MIMD multicomputer with 128 microprocessors and a logarithmic memory interconnection network.)

Borning, Alan (1979). "Thinglab: A Constraint-Oriented Simulation Laboratory," Stanford University Computer Science Department, Rep. 79-746;

also Xerox PARC Report SSL-79-3. (Shows what can be done with constraints. This is the modern version of Sutherland's SKETCHPAD.)

Bouknight, W. J., Stewart A. Denenberg, David E. McIntyre, J. M. Randall, Amed H. Sameh, and Daniel L. Slotnick (1972). "The Illiac IV System," *Proceedings of the IEEE* 60 (4): 369-388. (Overview of the Illiac IV, including software.)

Bracewell, R.N. (1984). "The Fast Hartley Transform," *Proceedings of the IEEE* 72 (8). (Gives fast version of transform FHT, similar to FFT. Included here because it shows a simple FFT program.)

Brachman, R.J. (1978a). "KLONE Reference Manual," BBN Report 3848, Bolt Beranek and Newman Inc., Cambridge, MA. (KLONE is probably the most developed knowledge representation language.)

Brachman, R.J. (1978b). "On the Epistemological Status of Semantic Networks," Rep. 3807, Bolt Beranek and Newman Inc., Cambridge, MA. (Background for KLONE.)

Broomell, George, and J. Robert Heath (1983). "Classification Categories and Historical Development of Circuit Switching Topologies," *Computing Surveys* 15 (2): 95-133. (A survey of interconnection topologies.)

Browning, S. A. (1980). "A Tree Machine," *Lambda Magazine* 1 (2): 31-36. (Overview of Tree Machine, mostly hardware.)

Buehrer, Richard E., Hans-Joerg Brundiers, Hans Benz, Bernard Bron, Hansmartin Friess, Walter Haelg, Hans Juergen Halin, Anders Isacson, and Milan Tadian (1982). "The ETH-Multiprocessor EMPRESS: A Dynamically Configurable MIMD System," *IEEE Transactions on Computers* C-31 (11): 1035-1044. (A 16-processor LSI-11 based MIMD multiprocessor, with (effectively) 16 16-port memories for communication. Describes parallelizing compiler for numeric simulation.)

Burks, Arthur W., Herman H. Goldstine, and John von Neumann (1946). "Preliminary Discussion of the Logical Design of an Electronic Computing Instrument," in *Report on the Mathematical and Logical Aspects of an Elec-*

tronic Computing Instrument, pt. I, vol. 1, The Institute for Advanced Study, ECP list of reports 1946–1957, no. 1. (Design document for "Johniac." Includes amusing estimate of maximum memory requirements.)

Cannon, H.I. (in preparation). "Flavors: A Non-hierarchical Approach to Object-Oriented Programming." (Would have been the standard "Flavors" reference if Howard had ever finished writing it. He didn't. See Weinreb and Moon (1980).)

Carroll, C.R. (1980). "Hardware Path Finders," *Caltech VLSI Conference Proceedings*, California Institute of Technology. (MAZER, routes circuit boards by distance-wave method. Carroll imagines a system with 1K by 1K cells.)

Chakravarthy, U. S., S. Kasif, M. Kohli, J. Minker, D. Cao (1982). "Logic Programming on ZMOB: A Highly Parallel Machine," Department of Computer Science, University of Maryland, College Park, MD, and *IEEE*. (Parallel prolog-like language on medium-grained MIMD machine with general communication.)

Chang, Hsu (1978). "Bubbles for Relational Database," *Fourth Annual Workshop on Computer Architecture for Non-Numeric Processing*, 110–115. (A brute-force database machine, including cartesian product and full join.)

Christman, David P. (1983). "Programming the Connection Machine," Master's Thesis, Department of Electrical Engineering and Computer Science, Massachusetts Institute of Technology. (Many good Connection Machine algorithms, including the first enumeration consing algorithms.)

Codd, E.F. (1972). "Relational Completeness of Data Base Sublanguages" in *Database Systems*, R. Rustin (ed.) Prentice Hall. (Compares the expressive power of various combination of primitives.)

Cole, G. C. (1971). "Computer Network Measurements: Techniques and Experiments," UCLA-ENG-7165. (A lot of measured and computed data on the Arpanet. Says buffer blocking is rare.)

Collins, A. M. and E. F. Loftus (1975). "A spreading activation theory of semantic processing," *Psychological Review* 82: 407–428. (See also Waltz and Pollack (1975) and Quillian (1968).

Comfort, W.T. (1963). "Highly parallel machines," in *Computer Organization*, Barnum (ed.), Spartan Books. (Talks about programming the Holland machine.)

Cooley, J.W., and J.W. Tukey (1965). "An Algorithm for the Machine Calculation of Complex Fourier Series," *Mathematics of Computation* 19: 297–301. (This is the paper that introduced the FFT. Easy to read.)

Copeland, G.P., G.J. Lipovski, and S.Y.W. Su (1973). "The Architecture of CASSM: A Cellular System for Non-numeric Processing," *Proceedings of the 1st Annual Symposium on Computer Architectures*, 121–128. (CASSM is a database machine. See Hawthorn and DeWitt (1982) for how it performed.)

Date, C. J. (1975). *An Introduction to Database Systems*, Addison-Wesley. (A good overview. Compares the various approaches.)

Davidson, Edward S. (1980). "A Multiple Stream Microprocessor Prototype System: AMP-1*," Coordinated Science Laboratory, University of Illinois, Urbana, IL, and *IEEE*. (Analysis of shared memory MIMD machine for matrix operations.)

de Kleer, J., Jon Doyle, Charles Rich, Guy L. Steele Jr, and Gerald Jay Sussman (1978). "AMORD: A Deductive Procedure System," Massachusetts Institute of Technology, Artificial Intelligence Laboratory Memo 435. (A working system that does truth maintenance.)

Dennett, D.C. (1978). *Brainstorms: Philosophical Essays on Mind and Psychology*, Bradford Books/MIT Press. (A discussion of some of the philosophical questions that arise in thinking of the mind as a computer or vice versa.)

Dennis, Jack B. (1980). "Data Flow Supercomputers," *Computer* (18): 42–56. (Introduces dataflow and compares fine-grained "cell-block" implementation to a more conventional multiprocessor implementation.)

Dennis, J.B., and K.S. Weng (1977). "Applications of Data Flow Computation to the Weather Problem," in *High Speed Computer and Algorithm Organization*, D.J. Kuck, D.H. Lawrie, and A. Sameh (eds.), Academic Press, 143–157. (An analysis of what specs would be needed for a Data Flow computer that could beat a IBM 360/195 by a factor of 100.)

DiGiacinto, Tom (1981). "Airborne Associative Processor (ASPRO)," Goodyear Aerospace Corporation, Akron, OH. (Like STARAN, see Batcher, 1974.)

Dongarra, J. J. (1984). "Performance of Various Computers Using Standard Linear Equations Software in a Fortran Environment," Technical Memorandum 23, Mathematics and Computer Science Division, Argonne National Laboratory, University of Chicago. (Contains a measured comparison of a wide variety of machines on a specific numeric application. Makes you want to go out and buy a Cray.)

Drescher, Gary L. (1980). "Suggestions for Genetic AI," Massachusetts Institute of Technology, Artificial Intelligence Laboratory, Working Paper 198. (Proposal for Drescher's learning program.)

Drescher, Gary L. (1985). "The Schema Mechanism: A Conception of Constructivist Intelligence," Master's Thesis, Massachusetts Institute of Technology. (Drescher's learning program is based on a model of human infants' cognitive development; derived from Piaget.)

Erdös, P., and A. Renyi (1959). "On Random Graphs I," *Publicationes Mathematicae* (Debrecen, Hungary) 6: 290–297. (Proves that to be connected a random graph needs an average degree of about $\frac{1}{2} ln N$ and that this is a sharp bound.)

Erdös, Paul, Frank Harary and William T. Tutte (1973). "On the Dimension of a Graph," in *Paul Erdös, The Art of Counting*, Paul Erdös and Joel Spencer (eds.), MIT Press. (Defines graph dimension according to minimum unit-length embedding in $E(n)$.)

Evans, T.G. (1968). "A program for the solution of geometric-analogy intelligence test questions," in *Semantic Information Processing*, M. Minsky (ed.), MIT Press. (An AI program that literally passed an IQ test.)

Fahlman, S.E. (1979). *NETL: A System for Representing and Using Real-World Knowledge*, MIT Press. (The thesis that inspired the Connection Machine.)

Fahlman, Scott E. (1981). "Design Sketch for a Million-Element NETL Machine," Department of Computer Science, Carnegie-Mellon University, Pittsburgh, PA. (A rough sketch of a NETL machine using off-the-shift rams, and telephone-style hookups.)

Feigenbaum, E. A., and Julian Feldman (eds.) (1963). *Computers and Thought*, McGraw-Hill. (A good early overview of AI.)

Feldman, J. A., and D. H. Ballard (1981). "Computing with Connections," TR7, Department of Computer Science, University of Rochester. (This is a good introduction to "connectionist" theories of AI. As might be guessed, they are well matched to implementation on the Connection Machine.)

Feller, William (1957). *An Introduction to Probability Theory and Its Applications*, 2 vols., Wiley. (The best general reference for probability. If you know it, it is probably there.)

Forster, Lyn (1982). "Vision and Prey-Catching Strategies in Jumping Spiders," *American Scientist*, March-April, 1982, 165–174. (Special purpose image processing hardware.)

Fried, David L. (1977). "Least-square fitting a wave-front distortion estimate to an array of phase-difference measurements," *Journal of the Optical Society of America* 67 (3): 370–375. (An example of a real-time control application that needs a Connection Machine.)

Friedman, Daniel P., and David S. Wise (1975). "An Environment for Multiple-Valued Recursive Procedures," Tech. Rep. 40, Indiana University Computer Science Department. (Another attempt to add vectorlike function calling to Lisp.)

Gajski, Daniel, David Kuck, Duncan Lawrie, and Ahmed Sameh (1983a).

"A Large Scale Multiprocessor," Laboratory for Advanced Supercomputers Cedar Project, Department of Computer Science, University of Illinois at Urbana-Champaign. (A short summary of the Cedar machine.)

Gajski, Daniel, David Kuck, Duncan Lawrie, and Ahmed Sameh (1983b). "Construction of a Large Scale Multiprocessor," Laboratory for Advanced Supercomputers Cedar Project, Department of Computer Science, University of Illinois at Urbana-Champaign. (Proposal to build Cedar, a 32 processor prototype of a machine similar to Ultra; uses an 8-way shuffle interconnection network.)

Garner, H.L., and J.S. Squire (1963). "Iterative Circuit Computers," in *Computer Organization*, Barnum (ed.), Spartan Books. (Compares *n*-cubes and 2-d grids for path building.)

Gerla, Mario (1973). "The Design of Store and Forward Networks for Computer Communications," PhD. Thesis, UCLA-ENG-7319. (Performance analysis, ignores buffer limitations.)

Gilmore, Paul A. (1982). "The Computer MPP," GER-17083, Defense Systems Division, Goodyear Aerospace Corporation, Akron, OH. (Another MPP overview.)

Goldberg, Adele, and David Robson (1983). *Smalltalk-80: The Language and Its Implementation*, Addison-Wesley. (One of the first languages based on message passing.)

Goldstine, Herman H., and John von Neumann (1948). "Planning and Coding of Problems for an Electronic Computing Instrument," *Report on the Mathematical and Logical Aspects of an Electronic Computing Instrument*, pt. II, vol. 2, The Institute for Advanced Study, Princeton, NJ. (Discussion of programming the "Johniac," including a merge sort.)

Goodman, J. R., and C. H. Sequin (1980). "Hypertree, A Multiprocessor Interconnection Topology," University of California at Berkeley. (An omega network augmented tree topology.)

Goodman, James R., and Alvin M. Despain (1981). "A Study of the Interconnection of Multiple Processors in a Data Base Environment," Computer Science Department, University of California, Berkeley, CA. (An analysis of interconnection topologies in the context of a specific database problem, the elimination of duplicates. Argues in favor of an augmented tree structure.)

Gottlieb, Allan, and J. T. Schwartz (1982). "Networks and Algorithms for Very-Large-Scale Computation," *Computer*, January 1982, 27–36. (A good introduction to paracomputers. See also Schwartz (1980b).)

Gottlieb, Allan, Ralph Grishman, Clyde P. Kruskal, Kevin P. McAuliffe, Larry Rudolph, and Marc Snir (1983). "The NYU Ultracomputer – Designing an MIMD Shared Memory Parallel Computer," *IEEE Transactions on Computers* C-32 (2): 175–189. (The hardware of a proposed 4096 processor ultracomputer, including detailed description and analysis of interconnection network.)

Gritton, E.C., W.S. King, I. Sutherland, R.S. Gaines, C. Gazley, Jr., C. Grosch, M. Juncosa, and H. Petersen (1977). "Feasibility of a Special-Purpose Computer to Solve the Navier-Stokes Equations," Rand Corp. r-2183-RC. (Sutherland (1965, pp. 22–28) suggests a 10K cell number cruncher for hydrodynamics problems.)

Gross, Donald, and Carl M. Harris (1974). *Fundamentals of Queueing Theory*, Wiley. (A good introduction. See also Kleinrock (1973, 1976).)

Halstead, R.H. (1979). "Reference Tree Networks: Virtual Machine and Implementation," MIT/LCS/TR-222, Massachusetts Institute of Technology, Laboratory for Computer Science, Cambridge, MA. (A neat programming idea for sharing data structures across multiple machines.)

Halstead, Robert H. Jr. and Stephen A. Ward (1980). "The Munet: A Scalable Decentralized Architecture for Parallel Computation," *Proc. 7th Annual Symposium on Computer Architectures*, 8 (3): 139-145. (A brief review of the Munet and reference trees. For more detail see Halstead's PhD. thesis.)

Harary, Frank (1969). *Graph Theory*, Addison-Wesley. (Best introduction to graph theory.)

Hawkins, J.K., and C.J. Munsey (1963). "A Two Dimensional Iterative Network Computing Technique And Mechanizations," in *Computer Organization*, Barnum (ed.), Spartan Books. (An optical 2-d grid computer.)

Hawthorn, Paula B., and David J. DeWitt (1982). "Performance Analysis of Alternative Database Machine Architectures," *IEEE Transactions on Software Engineering* SE-8 (1); 61–74. (Compares RAP, CASSM, DBC, DIRECT, and CAFS. If you plan to build a database machine, better read this first.)

Haynes, L.S., R.L. Lau, D.P. Sieqiorek, and D.W. Mizell (1982). "A Survey of Highly Parallel Computing," *Computer*, January 1982. (A good recent survey of parallel computing.)

Hendrix, Gary G. (1975). "Expanding the utility of semantic networks through partitioning," SRI Tech. Note 105. (Shows how to represent quantifiers in semantic networks through context mechanisms.)

Hewitt, C. (1969). "PLANNER: A Language for Proving Theorems in Robots," *International Joint Conference on Artificial Intelligence.* Washington, D.C., (69): 295–302. (One of the first high-level AI languages. See also Sussman (1972).)

Hewitt, C. (1977). "Viewing Control Structures as Patterns of Passing Messages," *Artificial Intelligence* 8 (3): 323–364. (Describes the ACTOR paradigm for describing computation.)

Hewitt, C. E. (1980). "The Apiary Network Architecture for Knowledgeable Systems," *Proceedings of Lisp Conference*, Stanford, 107–118. (A hardware architecture to support ACTORS.)

Hewitt C., G. Attardi, and M. Simi (1980). "Knowledge Embedding in the Description System Omega," *Proceedings of 1980 AAAI Conference*, Stanford, 157–164. (A provably consistent knowledge representation scheme.)

Hillis, W. Daniel (1981). "The Connection Machine," Massachusetts Institute of Technology Artificial Intelligence Laboratory Memo 646. (An early Connection Machine description.)

Hillis, W. Daniel (1982). "New Computer Architectures and Their Relationship to Physics or Why Computer Science Is No Good," *International Journal of Theoretical Physics* 21 (3/4): 255–262. (Shows why to expect computer science to begin to look like physics.)

Hillis, (W.) D. (1983). "Dynamics of Manipulators with Less Than One Degree of Freedom," Massachusetts Institute of Technology, Artificial Intelligence Laboratory, AI Working Paper 241. (A computation that cannot be speeded up by parallel processing.)

Hillis, W. Daniel (1984). "The Connection Machine: A Computer Architecture Based on Cellular Automata," *Physica* 10D: 213–228. (A slightly easier to find version of the AI memo.)

Hillis, W. Daniel, and Guy L. Steele Jr. (1985). *The Connection Machine Lisp Manual*, Thinking Machines Corporation, Cambridge, MA. (In preparation.)

Hoare, C.A.R. (1978). "Communicating Sequential Processes," *C.A.C.M.* 21 (8): 666–677. (An important paper, but a conservative approach to parallel programming.)

Hoffman, A. J., and R. R. Singleton (1960). "On Moore Graphs with Diameters 2 and 3," *IBM Journal*, November 1960, 497–504. (Moore graphs are optimal network topologies.)

Holland, John H. (1959). "A Universal Computer Capable of Executing an Arbitrary Number of Sub-Programs Simultaneously," *Proc. 1959 E.J.C.C.* 108–113. (This was one of the earliest proposed general purpose massively parallel computers.)

Holland, John H. (1960). "Iterative Circuit Computers," *Proceedings of Winter Joint Computer Conference, 1960* 259–265. (More on the Holland machine.)

Hopfield, J. J. (1982). "Neural Networks and Physical Systems with Emergent Collective Computational Abilities," *Proceedings of the National Academy of Sciences USA* (79): 2554–2558. (This is a new type of neural network learning model that fits well with the Connection Machine. This type of network was the first interesting progress in neural networks in many years.)

Jaffe, Jefffrey M. (1982). "Distributed Multi-Destination Routing: The Constraints of Local Information," IBM Research Report, RC 9243, IBM Corporation, Yorktown, NY. (Shows that local routing is fundamentally hard.)

Keller, Robert M., Gary Lindstrom, and Suhas Patil (1978). "An Architecture for a Loosely Coupled Parallel Processor," Tech. Rep. UUCS-78-105, Department of Computer Science, University of Utah, Salt Lake City, UT. (Description of a large-grain tree machine, and how to program it in LISP.)

Keller, Robert M., Gary Lindstrom, and Suhas Patil (1979). "A Loosely-Coupled Applicative Multi-Processing System," National Computer Conference, 613–622. (See Keller et al. (1978).)

Kirkpatrick, S., C.D. Gellatt, and M.P. Vecchi (1983). "Simulated Annealing," *Science* 220: 671. (Introduction to simulated annealing.)

Kleinrock, L. (1964). *Communications Nets: Stochastic Message Flow and Delay*, McGraw-Hill. (A classic, but assumes independence of message lengths and infinite buffers.)

Kleinrock, L. (1973). *Queueing Systems: Theory and Applications*, Wiley Interscience. (The basic text on queueing.)

Kleinrock, Leonard (1976). *Queueing Systems, Volume II: Computer Applications*, Wiley. (Volume II of above.)

Knight, T.F. (1983). "Design of an integrated optical sensor with on-chip preprocessing," PhD. Thesis, Massachusetts Institute of Technology. (A special-purpose vision processor that integrates the sensor onto the same chip as the processor. This is one trick the Connection Machine can't be programmed to do!)

Knuth, Donald E. (1968). *The Art of Computer Programming*, 3 vols., Addison-Wesley. (I am one of those people who keeps thinking, "One of these days I am going to sit down and read all of Knuth.")

Koton, P.A. (1980). "Simulating a Semantic Network in LMS," Bachelor's Thesis, Department of Electrical Engineering and Computer Science, Massachusetts Institute of Technology, Cambridge, MA. (Mentions problems with NETL.)

Kruskal, Clyde P., and Marc Snir (1982). "Some Results on Multistage Interconnection Networks for Multiprocessors," New York University, Computer Science Department, Tech. Rep. 51. (An analysis of Banyan networks and a specialization called delta network in which all path desceptors to a given destination are identical.)

Kuck, David J., and Richard A. Stokes (1982). "The Burroughs Scientific Processor (BSP)," *IEEE Transactions on Computers* C-31 (5): 363-376. (A fast Cray-class number cruncher, built but never produced.)

Kung, H.T., and P.L. Lehman (1980). "Systolic (VLSI) arrays for relational database operations," *International Conference on Management of Data*, May 1980. (Includes intersect, remove duplicates, union, join, divide.)

Kung, H.T., and C.E. Leiserson (1980). "Systolic Arrays," in *Introduction to VLSI Systems*, C.A. Mead and L.A. Conway, Addison-Wesley, sec. 8.3. (A good introduction to systolic arrays.)

Landauer, Rolf (1967). "Wanted: A Physically Possible Theory of Physics," *IEEE Spectrum* 4 (9): 105–109. (Is the universe a cellular automaton?)

Lang, T. and H.S. Stone (1976). "A Shuffle-Exchange Network with Simplified Control," *IEEE Transactions on Computers* C-25 (1): 55–65. (Introduction to shuffle exchange.)

Lawrie, D.H. (1975). "Access and Alignment of Data in an Array Processor," *IEEE Transactions on Computers* C-24 (12): 1145–1155. (Discusses omega networks.)

Lee, C.Y. (1962). "Intercommunicating Cells, Basis for a Distributed-Logic Computer," *Proceedings 1962 Fall Joint Computer Conference.* (A content addressable memory for string search.)

Lee, C.Y., and M.C. Paul (1963). "A Content-Addressable Distributed-Logic Memory with Applications to Information Retrieval," *IEEE Proceedings* 51: 924–932. (A local content addressable memory.)

Leiserson, Charles E. (1985). "FAT-TREES: Universal Networks for Hardware-Efficient Supercomputing," *1985 International Conference on Parallel Processing*, IEEE Computer Society, August 1985. (Fat trees are an augmented tree structure that gets thick toward the root. This paper shows the sense in which they are universal, that is, able to simulate efficiently any other physically realizable topology.)

Lieberman, Henry (1981). "Thinking About Lots of Things At Once Without Getting Confused: Parallelism in Act 1," AI Memo 626, Massachusetts Institute of Technology. (Act 1 is a language based on Actors.)

Lipovski, G.J. (1978). "Semantic Paging on Intelligent Discs," Fourth Annual Workshop on Computer Architecture for Non-Numeric Processing, 30–34. (Retrieval semantic nets by marker propagation, head-per-track-disks.)

Lundstrom, Stephen F., and George H. Barnes (1980). "A Controllable MIMD Architecture," *Proceedings of the International Conference on Parallel Processing*, 19-27. (Describes the FMP, a proposed architecture much like an ultracomputer designed for Navier-Stoke-type problems. Paper describes both hardware and software.)

Mago, Gyula A. (1979). "A Network of Microprocessors to Execute Reduction Languages, Part I," *International Journal of Computer and Information Sciences* 8 (5): 349–385. (This is a small-grained tree architecture, designed to implement Backus functional reduction language. See Backus (1978).)

Manning, F.R. (1975). "Automatic Test, Configuration and Repair of Cellular Arrays," MAC TR-151. (Shows how to repair defective grids.)

McDermott, D., and Gerald Sussman (1974). "The Conniver Reference Manual," Massachusetts Institute of Technology, Artificial Intelligence Laboratory Memo 259A. (A language that represents a peak in hairy control structure.)

Meadows, J.C. (1974). "The Anatomical Basis of Prosopagnosia," *Journal of Neurology, Neurosurgergy, and Psychiatry* 37: 489. (Evidence for special hardware for the recognition of faces.)

Metropolis, N., A. Rosenbluth, M. Rosenbluth, A. Teller, and E. Teller. (1953). *Journal of Chemical Physics* 21: 1807. (Describes the "Metropolis criterion" for accepting moves often used in simulated annealing.)

Michalski, R.S., and R.E. Flick (1983). "Automated Construction of Classifications: Conceptual Clustering Versus Numerical Taxonomy," *Pattern Matching and Machine Intelligence*, July 1983, 410–416. (A better form of cluster analysis and a good description of the problem. Allows three kinds of variables: nominal (symbols), numeric, and structured (trees) and clusters in hierarchy.)

Minsky, Marvin L. (1956). "Some Universal Elements for Finite Automata," in *Automata Studies*, C. E. Shannon and J. McCarthy (eds.), Princeton University Press, Princeton, NJ. (Besides the familiar stuff, shows that a neuron with a recovery time is universal.)

Minsky, M. (1961). "Steps Toward Artificial Intelligence," *Proc. IRE* 49 (1). Reprinted in Feigenbaum and Feldman 1963. (The best AI overview; an oldie but goodie.)

Minsky, M. (1967). *Computation: Finite and Infinite Machines*, Prentice-Hall. (A good introductory text on Turing machines, automata, etc.)

Minsky, M. (ed.) (1968). *Semantic Information Processing*, MIT Press. (Another AI classic.)

Minsky, M. (1974). "A Framework for Representing Knowledge," Massachusetts Institute of Technology, Artificial Intelligence Laboratory Memo 306. (This is the famous "frames" paper. It changed the way people thought about knowledge representation.)

Minsky, M. (1979). "*K*-Lines: A Theory of Memory," Massachusetts Institute of Technology Artificial, Intelligence Laboratory Memo 516. Reprinted in *Cognitive Science* (1980) 117–133. (A parallel memory theory that would work well on the Connection Machine.)

Minsky, M. (1980). "Jokes and the Logic of the Cognitive Unconscious," Massachusetts Institute of Technology, Artificial Intelligence Laboratory Memo 603. (One of the early "Society of Mind" papers.)

Minsky, M. (1982). "Learning Meaning," Massachusetts Institute of Technology, Artificial Intelligence Laboratory Memo. (New wave learning. See also Winston and Horn (1981).)

Minsky, M., and Seymour Papert (1969). *Perceptrons*, MIT Press; second edition, 1972. (Perceptrons were parallel learning machines. Anything that they could do, they could be taught to do by a simple algorithm. Unfortunately, they could not do much. This book seemed to put an end to them.)

Moon, David A. (1974). "MACLISP Reference Manual, Revision 0," Project MAC, Massachusetts Institute of Technology. (The Lisp on which Common Lisp in based.)

Moore, Edward F. (ed.) (1964). *Sequential Machines: Selected Papers*, Addison-Wesley. (Contains many of the original papers on sequential automata.)

Moore, E. F., and C. E. Shannon (1956). "Reliable Circuits Using Less Reliable Relays," *Journal of The Franklin Institute*, July-December, 1956. (Was originally called "Good Circuits with Crummy Relays." An elegant construction and analysis shows how arbitrarily reliable circuits can be constructed with arbitrarily unreliable switches.)

Moravec, Hans P. (1979). "Intelligent Machines: How to Get There From Here and What To Do Afterwards," Computer Science Department, Stanford University. (A fun but flaky paper comparing the human brain to a computer. Suggests the need for millions of times more raw power. Hans also published a very unflaky paper on parallel computers with sorting nets, but I can't find the reference. Hans?)

Newell, Allen, and Herbert A. Simon (1963). "GPS: a Program that Simulates Human Thought," in *Computers and Thought*, E. A. Feigenbaum and J. Feldman (eds.), McGraw Hill. (An AI classic, GPS is General Problem Solver, the basis for almost all problem solving programs.)

Omohundro, Stephen (1984). "Modelling Cellular Automata with Partial Differential Equations," *Physica* 10D 128–134. (This is the other side of what Wolfram is doing.)

Orcutt, Samuel E. (1976). "Implementation of Permutation Functions in Illiac IV-Type Computers," *IEEE Transactions on Computers* C-25 (9): 929–936. (How to do general communication on a grid.)

Ozkarahan, S. A., S. A. Schuster, and K. C. Sevcik (1974). "A Data Base Processor," Tech. Rep. CSRG-43, Computer Systems Research Group, University of Toronto. (The real scoop on RAP.)

Ozkarahan, S. A., S. A. Schuster, and K. C. Sevcik (1977). "Performance Evaluation of a Relational Associative Processor," *ACM Trans. Database Systems* 2 (2). (RAP, a working marker propagation system for relational databases, uses semi-joins.)

Papert, Seymour (1980). *Mindstorms*, Basic Books. (LOGO and why.)

Parhami, B. (1980). "Rapid: A Rotating Associative Processor for Information Dissemination," UCLA-ENG-7213, University of California, Los Angeles. (Like Lee CAM cells, fed from a disk.)

Parker, D. Stott, Jr (1980). "Notes on Shuffle/Exchange-Type Switching Networks," *IEEE Transactions on Computers* C-29 (3): 213–222. (Shows that indirect n-cube, omega network, and shuffle exchange are equivalent.)

Pease, M.C., III (1968). "An Adaptation of the Fast Fourier Transform for Parallel Processing," *Journal of the ACM* 15 (2): 252–264. (Discusses perfect shuffle.)

Pease, M.C., III (1977). "The Indirect Binary *n*-Cube Microprocessor Array," *IEEE Transactions on Computers* C-26: 458-473.

Peterson, W. Wesley, and E. J. Weldon, Jr. (1972). *Error-Correcting Codes*, MIT Press, second edition. (A good reference source for all types of error correction schemes.)

Quillian, M. Ross (1968). "Semantic memory," in *Semantic Information Processing*, M. Minsky (ed.), MIT Press, 227–270. (One of the first semantic networks with parallel marker propagation.)

Reeves, Anthony P. (1981). "Parallel Computer Architectures for Image Processing," *Proceedings of the International Conference on Parallel Processing*, 199-206. (A general review of SIMD grids, pipelined, and MIMD processors for vision.)

Rieger, C. (1979). "ZMOB: A Mob of 256 Cooperative Z80A-Based Microcomputers," Computer Science Tech. Rep. Series TR-825, University of Maryland, College Park, MD. (ZMOB is 256 280 processors tied together by a fast "conveyer belt" communications system.)

Rieger, C., John Bane, and Randy Trigg (1980). "ZMOB: A Highly Parallel Multiprocessor," Tech. Rep. TR-911, Department of Computer Science, University of Maryland, College Park, MD. (Tells detail of the ZMOB implementation, including a conveyer belt that rotates once every 10 μsec.)

Robertson, James E., and Kishor S. Trivedi (1973). "The Status of Investigations into Computer Hardware Design Based on the Use of Continued Fractions," *IEEE Transactions on Computers*, June 1973. (Describes continued fractions algorithms but not hardware for fractions restricted to powers of 2.)

Russell, R. M. (1978). "The Cray-1 Computer System," *Communications of the Association for Computing Machines* 21 (1): 63–72. (This is a good overview of the Cray-1 hardware.)

Schaefer, D. H., J. R. Fischer, and K. R. Wallgren (1982). "The Massively Parallel Processor," *Engineering Notes* 5 (3): 313–315. (More MPP.)

Schwartz, J. T. (1973). "On Programming, An Interim Report on the SETL Project," Computer Science Department, Courant Institute of Mathematical Science, New York University. (A programming language based on sets.)

Schwartz, Jacob T. (1980a). "The Burroughs FMP Machine," Ultracomputer Note #5, New York University, New York, NY. (Contains a good summary of the FMP routing algorithm. See Lundstrom and Barnes (1980).)

Schwartz, J. T. (1980b). "Ultracomputers," *ACM Transactions on Programming Languages and Systems* 2 (4): 484–521. (Lots of real content including short discussion of perfect-shuffle networks, many specific concurrent algorithms, a parallel programming language, and a great bibliography. One of the best papers on a parallel architecture.)

Schwartz, J. T. (1983). "A Taxonomic Table of Parallel Computers, Based on 55 Designs," Courant Institute, New York University. (This is a good overview of many existing and proposed parallel architectures. The discussion of parallel machines in chapter 1 follows this taxonomy.)

Seitz, Chuck (1980). "System Timing," chapter 7 of *Introduction to VLSI Systems*, Carver Mead and Lynn Conway, Addison-Wesley. (Discussion of synchronous versus asynchronous design and local synchronization.)

Sequin, Carlo H. (1981). "Doubly Twisted Torus Networks for VLSI Processor Arrays," Computer Science Division, University of California, Berkeley, CA. (A homogeneous two-dimensional topology.)

Sequin, C. H., and R. M. Fujimoto (1982). "X-Tree and Y-Components," Report UCB/CSD 82/107, Computer Science Division (EECS), University of California, Berkeley, CA. (Describes X-tree architecture with one-chip size PEs, ring augmented tree topology, and general 3-port buffered communications component that can be connected into different topologies.)

Sequin, C. H., A. M. Despain, and D. A. Patterson (1978). "Communication in X-Tree: A Modular Multiprocessor System," *Proceedings of ACM*, (12): 194-203. (Describes how a processor communicates in a ring augmented tree.)

Shannon, C. E. (1948). "A Mathematical Theory of Communication," *Bell System Technical Journal*, Monograph B-1598, vol. 27. (The original information theory paper.)

Shannon, Claude E. (1956). "A Universal Turing Machine with Two Internal States," in *Automata Studies*, C. E. Shannon and J. McCarthy (eds.), Princeton University Press, Princeton, NJ. (A neat construction shows how to simulate any Turing machine with one whose state machine has only two states.)

Shapiro, S.C., and M. Wand (1976). "The Relevance of Relevance," Indiana University CS Tech. Rep. 46. (Relevance logic, in which A implies B only if A was used to prove B.)

Shaw, David Elliot (1982). "The NON-VON Supercomputer," Department of Computer Science, Columbia University. (NON-VON is an almost-SIMD small-grained tree machine that has been built. This document includes a detailed description of both the hardware and the software.)

Shin, Kang G., Yann-Hang Lee, J. Sasidhar (1982). "Design of HM^2p — A Hierarchical Multimicroprocessor for General-Purpose Applications," *IEEE Transactions on Computers* C-31 (11): 1045-1053. (A proposed improvement on a CM*-type hierarchical multimicroprocessor.)

Sholl, D. A. (1956). *The Organization of the Cerebral Cortex*, Methuen. (Reverse engineering of the competition.)

Siegel, Howard Jay, Leah J. Siegel, Frederick C. Kemmerer, Philip T. Mueller, Jr., Harold E. Smalley, Jr., and S. Diane Smith (1981). "PASM: A Partitionable SIMD/MIMD System for Image Processing and Pattern Recognition," *IEEE Transactions on Computers* C-30 (12): 934-946. (PASM is a SIMD machine with a multiple microcontroller that can be partitioned to handle different parts of the array. The paper discusses both hardware and software.)

Slotnick, D.L., et al. (1978). "The ILLIAC IV Computer," *IEEE Transactions on Computers* C-17 (8): 746–757. (Overview of the first really big parallel machine.)

Small, Steven (1980). "Word Expert Parsing: A Theory of Distributed Word-Based Natural Language Understanding," Tech. Rep. 954, Department of Computer Science, University of Maryland. (A parallel processing view of how to understand language in which each word in the language needs it own computer. See also Waltz and Pollack (1985).)

Snir, Marc (1982). "Comments on Lens and Hypertrees — or the Perfect-Shuffle Again," Ultracomputer Note 38, Computer Science Department, New York University. (Shows that the de Brujn network mentioned in Goodman and Sequin (1980) is isomorphic to the shuffle exchange.)

Snyder, Lawrence (1982). "Introduction to the Configurable, Highly Parallel Computer," *Computer*, January 1982, 47-56. (Programmable systolic array in which the connection pattern can be set up to match an algorithm.)

Steele, Guy L. Jr. (1978). "Rabbit: A Compiler for Scheme," Massachusetts Institute of Technology, Artificial Intelligence Laboratory TR 474. (Shows how a compiler can get a lot of mileage by knowing about a few special constructs.)

Steele, Guy L. Jr. (1984). *Common LISP: The Language*, Digital Press. (The language on which CmLisp is built.)

Steele, Guy Lewis Jr., and Gerald Jay Sussman (1978). "The Revised Report on SCHEME: A Dialect of Lisp," AI Memo 452, Massachusetts Institute of Technology. (The lisp on which Common Lisp should have been based. Includes lexical scoping, full funarg, and cleaner syntax and uses value cell for function bindings.)

Stefik, Mark (1981). "Planning with Constraints (Molgen: Part 1)," *Artificial Intelligence* 16: 111–139. (An AI program that actually did something useful. A good example of an expert system.)

Stefik, Mark, et al. (1982). "The Organization of Expert Systems: A Prescriptive Tutorial," VLSI-82-1, Xerox Palo Alto Research Centers. (A good overview of methods.)

Stolfo, Salvatore J., and David Elliot Shaw (1982). "DADO: A Tree-Structured Machine Architecture for Production Systems," Department of Computer Science, Columbia University. (Dado is a MIMD tree machine, designed specifically for production systems.)

Sullivan, H., and T. R. Bashkow (1977). "A Large Scale, Homogeneous, Full Distributed Parallel Machine I," *Proceedings of 4th Annual Symposium on Computer Architecture* 105–117.

Surprise, Jon M. (1981). "Airborne Associative Processor (ASPRO)," *Proceedings of the International Conference on Parallel Processing*, 129-130. (STARAN in a shoebox.)

Sussman, Gerald Jay, and Drew McDermott (1972). "Why Conniving is Better than Planning," Massachusetts Institute of Technology, Artificial Intelligence Laboratory Memo 255A. Reprinted in *Proc FJCC* 41: 1171–1179. (An argument for hairy control structure.)

Sussman, Gerald Jay, and Guy L. Steele Jr. (1980). "Constraints: A Language for Expressing Almost-Hierarchical Descriptions," *Artificial Intelligence* 14: 1–39. "Constraints," an earlier version of this article was published in 1978 by Massachusetts Institute of Technology, Artificial Intelligence Laboratory Memo 502A. (A good introduction to programming by constraints.)

Sutherland, I.E. (1965). "SKETCHPAD: A Man Machine Graphical Communications System," Massachusetts Institute of Technology, Lincoln Laboratory Tech. Rep. 296. (This is the original constraint programming system.)

Swan, R. J., S. H. Fuller, and D. P. Siewiorek (1977). "Cm* — A Modular, Multi-Microprocessor," *Proc. AFIPS Conf.*, (46): 637-643. (Good review of Cm*, one of the first multiprocessors actually built. Uses multiple PDP-11's in a mapped bus hierarchy.)

Szolovitz, P., L. Hawkinson, and W. A. Martin (1977). "An Overview of OWL, a Language for Knowledge Representation," MIT/LCS/TM-86, Massachusetts Institute of Technology, Laboratory for Computer Science, Cambridge, MA. (OWL is another knowledge representation language with some attempt to define the semantics.)

Tenenbaum, Eric (1983). "A Comparison of Parallel Computer Architectures for AI Applications," Bachelor's Thesis, Massachusetts Institute of Technology. (Compares the Connection Machine to DADO.)

Thompson, Clark D. (1978). "Generalized Connection Networks for Parallel Processor Intercommunication," *IEEE Transactions on Computers*, C-27 (12). (Gives $7.6 \log N$ general connection network, summarizes other work on general connection networks, and shows how to go from a general connection network or permutation network to a routing scheme for broadcasts or shuffles.)

Thompson, Clark D. (1979). "Area-Time Complexity for VLSI," *11th Annual ACM Symposium on the Theory of Computing*. (Introduces a model of computation based on communication bandwidths between partitions.)

Toffoli, Tommaso (1977). "Cellular Automata Mechanics," Tech. Rep. 208, Logic of Computers Group, CCS Department, The University of Michigan. (Physicslike behavior in cellular automata.)

Treleaven, P. C., and G. F. Moll (1980). "A Multi-Processor Reduction Machine for User-Defined Reduction Languages," *Seventh Annual Symposium on Computer Architecture*, La Baule, France, 121–130. (A machine for executing functional languages.)

Trivedi, Kishor S. (1977). "On the Use of Continued Fractions for Digital Computer Arithmetic," *IEEE Transactions on Computers*, July 1977, 700–704. (Describes continued fractions algorithms but not hardware for fractions restricted to powers of 2.)

Trujillo, Vito A. (1982). "System Architecture of a Reconfigurable Multimicroprocessor Research System," *1982 International Conference on Parallel Processing*. (MIMD machine with a 20×32 processor-to-memory crossbar.)

Turing, Alan M. (1950). "Can a Machine Think?" *Mind*, October 1950, 433–460. Reprinted in Feigenbaum and Feldman (1963). (A classic, introduces the "Turing Test.")

Turner, D. A. (1979a). "A New Implementation Technique for Applicative Languages," *Software — Practice and Experience* vol. 9, 31–49. (Combinators, a "curried" version of lambda calculus that eliminates the need for symbol binding. Combinators can be reduced (evaluated) locally and in parallel, so they make an interesting model of parallel computation. Combinator hackers: this paper introduces some new combinators, besides S-K-I, that help keep the translation from blowing up in space.)

Turner, D. A. (1979b). "Another Algorithm for Bracket Abstraction," *The Journal of Symbolic Logic* 44 (2): 267–270. (An algorithm for translating applicative expressions into combinators. See Turner (1979a).)

Valiant, L. G. (1982a). "A Scheme for Fast Parallel Communication," *SIAM Journal on Computing* 11 (2): 350-361. (Probabilistic limited-storage routing algorithm for an n-cube.)

Valiant, L. G. (1982b). "Optimality of a Two-Phase Strategy for Routing in Interconnection Networks," TR-15-82, Aiken Computation Laboratory, Center for Research in Computing Technology, Harvard University, Cambridge, MA. (Describes Valiant randomization method for reducing worst case to twice the random case.)

von Neumann, John (1945). "First Draft of a Report on the EDVAC," University of Pennsylvania Report for the U.S. Army Ordinance Department. (This is the original design document for the "von Neumann Machine," and this report is why it got credited to him. J.P. Eckert and J. W. Mauchly were responsible for many of the ideas presented.)

von Neumann, John (1958). *The Computer and the Brain*, Yale University Press. (A classic. A series of lectures about the von Neumann Computer, and why.)

von Neumann, John (1956). "Probabilistic Logics and the Synthesis of Reliable Organisms From Unreliable Components," *Automata Studies*, C. E.

Shannon and J. McCarthy (eds.), Princeton University Press, Princeton, NJ. (A brute-force neural-net voting scheme. Lacks elegance, and requires lots of redundancy, but it works for any sort of error. A classic.)

von Neumann, John (1966). "Theory and Organization of Complex Automata," lecture delivered at the University of Illinois, December, 1949. Published in *Theory of Self-Reproducing Automata*, University of Illinois Press, 1966. (History. Fun to read.)

Waltz, David L., and Jordan B. Pollack (1985). "Massively Parallel Parsing: A Strongly Interactive Model of Natural Language Interpretation," *Cognitive Science* 9 (1): 51–74. (A relaxation network algorithm for interpreting natural language. Each word in the language effectively uses its own process element, so the interpretation is done concurrently. Very neural-networkish. I like it. See also Small (1980).)

Ward, S. A. (1978). "The MuNet: A Multiprocessor Message-Passing System Architecture," *Seventh Texas Conference on Computing Systems*, Houston, Texas. (Short overview of MuNet.)

Weinreb, Daniel, and David A. Moon (1980). "Flavors: Message Passing in the Lisp Machine," Massachusetts Institute of Technology, Artificial Intelligence Laboratory Memo 602. (Flavors is a programming system based on message passing. See also Cannon (in preparation).)

White, Steve R. (1984). "Concepts of Scale in Simulated Annealing," RC 10661, IBM Thomas J. Watson Research Center, Yorktown Heights, NY. (My favorite paper on simulated annealing. Lots of content on what temperatures to use when.)

Widdoes, L.C. (1980). "The S-1 Project: Developing High Performance Digital Computers," Spring COMPCON 1980, 282–291. (The S-1 is a big hairy machine that was designed to be used in clusters of 16 with a shared memory. The project was a source of lessons, good and bad, for the Connection Machine project.)

Wiener, Norbert (1948). *Cybernetics: Or Control and Communication in the Animal and the Machine*, MIT Press. (An introduction to the field that begat artificial intelligence and understanding of servomechanisms.)

Williams, Michael D. (1978). "The Process of Retrieval from Very Long Term Memory," CHIP 75, University of California, San Diego. (Bartlett-like sudy of high school yearbook name recall.)

Winston, Patrick H. (1980). "Learning and Reasoning by Analogy," Massachusetts Institute of Technology, Artificial Intelligence Laboratory Memo 520. (An example of the new wave of learning programs that will need the Connection Machine.)

Winston, Patrick H., and Berthold K. P. Horn (1981). *Lisp*, Addison-Wesley. (A good overview of Lisp.)

Wittie, Larry D. (1981). "Communication Structures for Large Networks of Microcomputers," *IEEE Transactions on Computers* C-30 (4): 264–273. (Dual-bus hypercubes.)

Wolfram, Stephen (1984). "Cellular Automata as Models of Complexity," *Nature* 311 (4): 419–424. (Prettier pictures than the IAS version.)

Wolfram, Stephen (1984a). "Cellular Automata: Towards a Paradigm for Complexity," The Institute for Advanced Study, Princeton, NJ. (Models of complexity that are appropriate for parallel processing.)

Wolfram, Stephen (1984b). "Twenty Problems in the Theory of Cellular Automata," The Institute for Advanced Study, Princeton, NJ. (If you want to work on cellular automata, read this.)

Woods, W. A. (1975). "What's in a Link? Foundations for Semantic Networks," in *Representation and Understanding: Studies in Cognitive Science*, D. G. Bobrow and A. M. Collins (eds.), Academic Press (1975), 35–82. (A good discussion of the semantics of semantic networks.)

Woods, W.A. (1978). "Research in Natural Language Understanding: Progress Report No. 2," Report 3797, Bolt Beranek and Newman Inc., Cambridge, MA. (Talks about a version of marker propagation using subscripted markers. Halfway to pointers.)

Woods, W.A. (1979). "Research in Natural Language Understanding: Progress Report No. 6," Report 4181, Bolt Beranek and Newman Inc., Cambridge, MA. (More on subscripted markers.)

Wu, Shyue B., and Ming T. Liu (1981). "A Cluster Structure as an Interconnection Network for Large Multimicrocomputer Systems," *IEEE Transactions on Computers* C-30 (4): 254-264. (Analytic comparison of tree, hierarchy, and hypercube.)

Zeigler, J. F. (1971). "Nodal Blocking in Large Networks," UCLA-ENG-7167, University of California, Los Angeles. (Blocking in grids.)

Index

–H–

–G–